Eight *New* Commodity Technical Trading Methods

Eight *New* Commodity Technical Trading Methods

by J.D. Hamon

Windsor Books, Brightwaters, N.Y.

Published by Windsor Books
P. O. Box 280
Brightwaters, N.Y. 11718

Manufactured in the United States of America

CAVEAT: It should be noted that all commodity trades, patterns, charts, systems, etc., discussed in this book are for illustrative purposes only and are not to be construed as specific advisory recommendations. Further note that no method of trading or investing is foolproof or without difficulty, and past performance is no guarantee of future performance. All ideas and material presented are entirely those of the author and do not necessarily reflect those of the publisher or bookseller.

In appreciation
I wish to thank my office help
especially, Stephanie Curry and Catherine Parker.
Also, William Spear of E.F. Hutton in Houston
for his many good suggestions.
Of course, my wife Barbara Hamon,
whose cooperation made this possible.
I am also grateful to Dr. J.T. Wilson
whose testing and computer programming
has been most gratifying these past three years.

TABLE OF CONTENTS

Problems of Processors and Middlemen...Hedging Influences...
Meaning of Front-Month Back-Month Changes...The Raw
Material of the Technician...What Others Have Done...What We
Consider Most Important...Theory Used...Some Measurements
Of The Market...What This Adds Up To...How To Use Price,
Volume, And Open Interest...What Are The Possibilities?...
Genie Trading Method

The Best Way To Make Money...What Others Have Done In This
Area of Work...What Are Pivot Finder Lines (PFL)?...How To
Find The Pivot Finder Lines...Getting The Lines Right...Make
Transparent Overlays...How To Make The Transparent Overlay...
Instruction For Use Of The Pivot Finder Overlay...How To Use
Pivot Finder Lines...Summary of Use For Pivot Finder Lines...
Trading Strategy

What Are Widgets and Toes?...What the Widgets Do...Types of
Widget Lines...Kinds of Widgets...Working the Widgets...HAP'S
Widgets Use...Ways To Use The Widgets

Staying Out of Trouble...The Part That Really Counts...Why Only
Part Of Market Action Is Important For Long Term Trades...
What This Means To The Long Term Trader...What The Long
Term Trader Needs To Know...What Others Have Done To Solve
This Problem...What Is Vital...The Kinds of Markets Involved...
How HAP Finds Accumulation and Distribution...The Pressure
Index of HAP...Calculating the Pressure Index (First Way)...
How To Use The Pressure Index...The Pressure Chart

Theory Used on Median Lines...Rules For Trading The Median
Lines...F.F.E.S.—Reverse Median Lines

Theory Used...How To Find The Rhythm Count...Where This
Originated...How To Trade With The Rhythm Method...Value
Of Using Rhythm

Why Closes Are More Important...What Is Expected In Closeline
Trading...What Others Have Done...Theory Behind The Closeline
Method...How To Use In Trading...Program For Trading The
''Closeline''

FIGURES

INTRODUCTION

There is much difference of opinion about what comprises a good trading plan. Some people want to use their own judgment in their trading method, and others want to be told exactly what to do. The mathematically inclined want formulas and equations, but price pattern traders do not trust formulas. Fundamentalists think they have the answer, but technicians seldom pay any attention to fundamentals. Some try to take a middle position: mixing formulas, fundamentals, and technical aspects.

Thousands of brokers and trading advisors are advertising that they have the answer. With so many claiming to have the right answer, why do so many traders lose? Call almost any broker or advisor and hear how great they are doing and why you ought to deal with them. It is said the way to make money in the market is to find someone bragging about his market analysis, then do the opposite. The Bullish Consensus trades opposite the advice of most advisors.

It is not unusual for an otherwise intelligent person to spend years trying to find some special formula to beat the market. In our files hidden away are special secret formulas given to us with the admonition not to let anyone know about them. They cannot be used for fear of violating a confidence—but are not of much value anyway. The market cannot be boiled down to one secret formula. However, technical analysis will help if a trader knows the proper way to use it.

Remember that markets are people's actions. Few people live by a formula. Some may run their business by a set of rules, but this is based on what other people do. A market formula that does not consider the nature of people will undoubtedly fail. There can be formulas to judge strength, cycle length, or various facets of market analysis, but these are all altered by the human element involved in trading. There are influences and conditions that cause people to act, but few people do the same thing when given the same set of circumstances. So how can trading be reduced to a mechanical method? People aren't mechanical! It is a test of skill and ability to best judge the most likely actions of people. By learning all that is possible about the market, you will be able to trade with greater skill than the opponent who may take your money.

How a person trades must depend upon the time he has for analysis and the amount of money he has for speculation. Personal judgment in a trading plan cannot be eliminated by the small trader. He logically must learn the skills and techniques that will make him better than those he trades against, or he will lose. This book is dedicated to helping you become a winner. This work should give you more ability as a trader and put new methods in your "toolkit".

CHAPTER 1

VIOLA GENIE

Note: The Viola Genie system is meant as a base—a set of tools from which you can develop your own system. It is not meant to be a fully defined trading system.

PROBLEMS OF PROCESSORS AND MIDDLEMEN

Those in the animal fattening business have more than changing prices to worry about. They must be concerned also with the changing price of feed and other rising costs. In situations where operators borrow money to finance their business, the rising costs of financing may also be a problem. It is known how much feed will be needed to produce each extra pound of meat, but it is not known when workers will strike for higher wages or when transportation costs will go up. More risk is involved than most people realize. It is like "wildcatting" for oil. There must be unusually good profit potential to tempt a person to risk his money. Many people complain about the middlemen, but few would venture their money with the risks involved.

The feeder businessman may have to hedge against rising feed costs as well as declining meat prices. The feeder cows have been purchased at a price to allow profits, but these can be wiped out by rising costs. There may be enough feed on hand for the ordinary length of feeding, but, if the owner must wait for a breakeven price to sell, more feed will be needed. With interest rates moving up steadily, he may need to hedge against rising interest rate costs. If he is hoping to market his product overseas, the rate of exchange of this currency against the dollar must be considered. It is possible that four different hedges, all costing money, would have to be used; one for the changing price of his product, one for changing feed costs, one for interest rates and the fourth for the falling value of the dollar. With all these risks, it is a wonder that we have any processors. Yet, there is a constant cry of the public against the middleman who is supposed to be bilking the public. This should give you an idea why only very good profits can get venture capital into these businesses.

HEDGING INFLUENCES

The above paragraph should help the trader better understand why hedging is necessary. The commercial's survival depends upon his ability in the futures market. There is a constant shifting of spreaders or hedgers between the front months and the back months. By front months we mean the first two. Back months are any actively traded ones beyond this. Since the front months are closer to actual delivery, they are more sensitive to change. Long term positions may be taken in the back months, with the front months used for offsetting losses incurred in a short term swing by taking an opposite position in the front months (hedging).

About ten years ago, Bill Ohama noticed he fluctuations of the front months and back months of commodities and did some research, which led to his 3-D method. When prices go down, the back months would be the most likely to first start rising since they have more time for the possible future change that may mean a profit. On the other hand, the front months would normally be the first to change in reversing cash markets since they run out the quickest. It is the usual procedure for the Bull spreaders to be short the back months, and the Bears to be short the front months. The contract running out the quickest is the one that is used to go with the prevailing trend. Interest rate changes affect the back months more. If the price of the futures is higher than the stored product, the futures market is shorted to assure a profit.

MEANING OF FRONT-MONTH BACK-MONTH CHANGES

1. If front months are going down in price more than back months and if open interest is increasing faster on the back months, this could mean that the commercials are pessimistic and shorting the market or hedging the futures against their cash product. The price, volume and open interest of the front months need to be compared with the back months of a commodity to understand this condition.

2. By watching the volume and open interest, as well as the price changes of back months in comparison with the front months, patterns of repetition emerge to enable a trader to make profits.

3. The spot months may be full of traders hoping for a squeeze before delivery. When there is a preponderance of traders, the well-funded stay in the market, knowing that prices will often take a sharp turn when speculators are getting out.

4. Large positions taken in back months may be rolled over to new back months as they become front months. It pays to keep tabs on the back-month, front-month relationship.

5. If the market is going down, watch the back months to see if they follow, or perhaps even go up some. If the market is going up, watch for a faster change of several months that are ahead of the changes of the rest of the months. A plan of action to do this is given near the end of this chapter.

THE RAW MATERIAL OF THE TECHNICIAN

All the technician has to work with is price, volume and open interest. A number of analysts have taken these three to form trading plans they proclaim to be winners.

WHAT OTHERS HAVE DONE

1. Index of Price, Volume, and Open Interest
Take the difference in price for the day, or week, convert this into dollar amounts (according to how it trades), multiply this times volume, then add or subtract the open interest change for the day or week according to math rules of positive or negative on an up or down market.

Viola Genie

2. A Take-Off From the Comparative Index Method

The Comparative Index compares a commodity with its complex. These same principles are used by some; but, instead of comparing a commodity complex with one of its members, the Comparative Index compares one interpretive factor with a combination of other interpretive factors. For instance, compare price against a moving average that combines price, volume and open interest. The combination of differing factors can be achieved by normalizing to get percentages, which can then be combined. The current amount or sum then can be divided by the moving average of the total normalized sum to make an oscillator.

3. Combinations Of The Above

Various formulas have been tried for combining volume, open interest, and price to make a predictive tool. Using up or down amounts of price, volume, and open interest, there can be a number of different techniques worked out to make indexes or oscillators.

4. What We Use In This Method

The *Viola Genie* method separates the front months and back months for comparison using 3-D techniques for signals. (See pg. 72.) Volume and open interest are used only when a significant change has been made. Moving averages of volume and open interest are used to make a price prediction, as well as two oscillators to compare with each other and with price.

WHAT WE CONSIDER MOST IMPORTANT

1. Volume, when there has been at least a thirty percent increase.
2. Front-month, back-month comparisons using the Ohama 3-D concept.
3. Open interest, if it has had a recent five percent change, or if it has made a recent three percent up-then-down move.
4. Short term cycle timing periods for tying these together.
5. Use of a special formula uniting Comparative Index principles with cycles, 3-D techniques, and price projection methods to make a superb predictive tool.

THEORY USED

1. The Comparative Index

If all the grains are averaged, then one of the grains is compared with the average. This is called the Comparative Index method, as mentioned earlier.

2. Comparative Index Variations

A step beyond this is to combine all the measurements of price action into one average and judge current price as compared to this average of several factors. According to our records, Jim Sibett was the first to propose this method. In order to transfer price, volume, and open interest into one common denominator, they are each normalized, then added or subtracted according to whether or not they are plus or minus. To normalize, the latest sum in a moving average can be divided by the moving average. This reduces the amounts to a percent that can be used in equations.

SOME MEASUREMENTS OF THE MARKET

1. The price for each month of a contract is most important. Much work has been done using only price. Spread relationships reveal the strength or weakness of a market. Front-month, back-month comparisons help. Old highs, lows or congestion areas give clues for support or resistance. The speed of price can be compared with average angles. Other price-time relationships can be used.

2. Next is volume for the day, or week. The problem is trying to decide what part of the total volume can be attributed to day traders and spreaders moving in and out. If a contract is changed from May to July, this is volume but has a different predict ve value. The action of day traders and floor specialists for the exchanges appears in volume, but usually does not apply to predictive tools for those trading more than a day.

To find the usefulness of volume, make a moving average, then when the current volume amount is thirty percent (more or less) than the moving averages, use this as an indicator to trade.

3. Open interest is different from volume. Unless a trade is kept overnight it is not counted on open interest. Moving from one month to another does not affect the over all total of open interest. Our research

shows that there must be a sharp change in open interest before there is any predictive value. Buyers think prices are going up, sellers think they are going down; open interest increases, but price may stay about the same depending on how aggressive one side may be. Increase or decrease in open interest is not predictive by itself unless price change and volume is also considered.

Price going up with increasing open interest means the buyers are more aggressive than sellers. Price going down with open interest decreasing means that there are aggressive sellers.

If price goes up with open interest going down, those getting out are covering shorts and not rolling over or reversing. Shorts and sellers taking profits must buy to offset their short positions. The reverse is true if open interest is down and price is down; longs are selling and shorts are covering. To get out, longs must go short and shorts must go long. There are seasonal changes in open interest that also must be considered.

WHAT THIS ADDS UP TO

To analyze these circumstances, the only time open interest changes are important is when the buyers are more aggressive than sellers or vice-versa. Short or long covering signals the realization of a mistake, and also reveals that the investors do not think enough of their convictions to reverse. The only time open interest is of any value is when it is going down or up much faster than normal.

Sharply rising open interest is often considered bearish because large commercials or hedgers are more apt to be short. But if there is an explosive runaway market, this is not true.

Sharply falling open interest is generally considered bullish since this implies that the large commercials are getting out preparing to go short again at some high level.

HOW TO USE PRICE, VOLUME, AND OPEN INTEREST

1. Make moving averages of prices, volume and open interest the length of the short cycle time period for a front month and a back month of a commodity. Use the front month contract with largest open interest and back month contract of largest open interest.

2. Normalize each of these by dividing the current days amount by the moving averages.

3. Only use volume as a signal to buy or sell when it is thirty percent above or below the moving average.

4. Only use open interest signals when there is a five percent change within a five day period, and also only after there have been volume changes that are more than thirty percent of the averages.

5. Arrive at the new sum to be normalized by adding or subtracting according to whether or not the sum is plus or minus, counting up-days as plus. Get a total percent for both front months and back months.

6. When volume is not thirty percent above or below the moving average, use the last number over again.

7. When open interest is not five percent greater in the past five days, use the last sum again.

8. Plot these two oscillators under price where they show their relationship with each other as well as with price.

9. For Trading

    a. Use Ohama's 3-D methods (See pg. 72.)

    b. Note divergence from the price chart.

    c. Use trend lines on oscillators (the oscillators are made by dividing the current figure by the moving average).

10. Combine by taking the moving average of the small cycle length used in comparison with the current price (or volume, or open interest). Now divide the data for the new day by the moving average amount for that day. Be sure to keep track of the plus or minus signs and record them correctly according to the principles of algebra. When using volume, take the total volume of all months and divide it by the number of days of the short cycle to get the average for that number of days. Now divide the amount of volume for that day by the moving average sum for the day to normalize. This compares the current amount with the moving average.

Do not use the spot month, nor any month with less than three hundred contracts in open interest. Average the price of the front month, then the back month. Make two sets of calculations to end up with two oscillators.

If the only volume amounts available are for all the months, a percentage of total open interest must be obtained and used to estimate the volume for each month.

You may be able to get your broker to give you the per contract amounts of volume. If this is to be kept current, estimated amounts must be used as furnished by the wire services or from the exchanges. Usually it is sufficient to work a day behind.

Do not forget that with the open interest you will be using the differences only. The total change for the moving average of the small cycle period is averaged, then the current day's change is divided by the average.

To make things quicker to record, make up a legend using an abbreviated symbol to denote each statistic. Below is an example of a suggested legend:

FAP	= Front Average Price
FAV	= Front Average Volume
BAP	= Back Average Price
BAV	= Back Average Volume
FPMA	= Front Price Moving Average
BPMA	= Back Price Moving Average
FVMA	= Front Month Volume Moving Average
BVMA	= Back Month Volume Moving Average
FOIC	= Front Month Open Interest Average Change
BOIC	= Back Month Open Interest Average Change
FOIMA	= Front Month Open Interest Moving Average
BOIMA	= Back Month Open Interest Moving Average

WHAT ARE THE POSSIBILITIES?

1. Price

a. If the front month is up and the back month down, then the commercials may be buying back their front contracts and selling back ones. There could also be increased selling in the back months. This can lead to down action in both front and back months because the commercials should not be interested in reversing in the front months they are vacating. The market should go down, as the public and floor traders will probably not make up the difference. This should not last long, however, as the public cannot stand a big loss and will soon exit.

b. If one or more of the front months makes new highs, whereas the back does not, this is a sign of weakness; if other indicators agree, sell the month that does not make new highs. If one or more contracts fail to make new lows, when the remaining contracts make new lows, buy the month that has not made new lows if other indicators agree.

c. The spot contract may not make new highs because of weakness in the cash product, so this cannot be considered as an indication.

d. When the price is in a carrying charge market, with each contract lower than the next older contract, the major trend is usually up. If price is in a cash premium market, with each contract higher than its next older contract, the major trend could be either up or down, as this is normal. The further off months should be higher due to carrying charges.

e. This work can be done between closely related commodities to make these same comparisons.

2. Volume

Two record volume days with higher closes in a weak market is considered a buy signal.

After a sharp drop in price, with record volume on several days, a higher outside day is considered a reversal day.

3. Open Interest

Open interest is only used in connection with price and volume. When volume makes several record high days, it is important to know if this volume is composed of traders staying in the market or just day trading. If there is only a small change in open interest on the high-volume days, this will mean that the volume is merely day traders. But if open interest increases one percent and better still, three percent, this means that the high volume is composed of more than just scalpers.

GENIE TRADING METHOD

1. If price is about a 3 day Moving Average, (leave an option as some may want as much as a 20 day Moving Average) and if Volume is up 30 percent above a 10 day Moving Average, and if Open Interest is up 3 percent from the previous day, **this is a trade indication.**

2. If price is above the Moving Average but Volume is not 30 percent above the Moving Average, do not count the Open Interest and this is a **zero day, or no trade indication.** Wait for price to go above or below the Moving Average for the first signal.

The exceptions are:

a. If Open Interest has recently had a one percent increase for 3 days, then followed by a 3 percent decrease, making an up and down bump on the O.I. line: if this happens, give a lot of weight to any reversal indications.

   b. If Open Interest has in the last 15 days gone down 30 percent, this will add extra weight to a buy signal. If short already, bring in the stops close, because a reversal is expected.

   3. If price closes below a 3 day Moving Average, (or whatever length desired by trader) and if Volume is up 30 percent above a 10 day Moving Average (or length of Moving Average chosen), and if Open Interest is up 3 percent, **this is a strong indication to go short.**

   4. If price closes below the Moving Average without Volume or Open Interest confirming, **it is a zero day** unless the exceptions come in. Further confirmation is needed by:

   a. Short Cycles being within 2 days time due for a change.

   b. Four contract months all giving a signal. The four months to pick must meet the following guidelines:

   Months with the most open interest;

   No months with under 300 contracts outstanding;

   Never use the spot month.

   5. Must have a new low, lower than any low of the last eight days, or a new high, higher than any high of the last eight days.

   6. What is being done: We are using Price Reversal, Volume, Open Interest, Cycles, Bubble Theory and Ohama's 3-D Method to confirm a trade

   7. Congestion: any time price swings between two opposite points of a trading range at least twice. Here we must trade differently. Usually just count signals as at top going down, or on bottom going up to tell if there is accumulation. If two signals occur on bottom or top enter when price comes back the third time.

   8. Getting out, if no reversal signal.

   a. The first 5 days use a crossover of a 5 day Moving Average.

   b. After this, if not in a Congestion area, use 10 day Moving Average.

   c. Bring back to 5 day Moving Average when near the short cycle time change.

   9. Expect the fourth attempt at going through a support or resistance area to succeed. For example: when in a Congestion area, do not buy or sell on the fourth attempt to come through the bottom or go through the top. Only buy or sell the third attempt. If you do, and the market comes back to your entry area, get out at break-even and look for signals to reverse.

10. Number of days data to use for testing when getting started.

    a. 101 days Maximum and

    b. 31 days Minimum.

    c. Reason for odd days is that on daily updating, the first day's data will not be accurate for Volume and Open Interest changes.

CHAPTER 2

PIVOT FINDER LINES

THE BEST WAY TO MAKE MONEY

The best way to make money in the market is to find things that repeat. This is a constant effort for traders because the market changes every week. As new formulas or techniques are discovered, old techniques are fading away. The market reflects life; there is a constant process of new life coming on, with an aging or fading of the old. Basic rules and information do not change; but since this is a one against one game of humans, abilities of traders change. For example, seasonals are considered a reliable indicator; but when too many use this, the smart trader starts trading against it to make money.

Various techniques gain or lose popularity among traders. One smart trader learned that the big traders usually bought on a certain day of the week. After they placed their orders for several days, this pushed the market their way. All the smart trader had to do was note the way the market went the day after the big traders bought, and trade with this move, taking a slice out of the market. Eventually, the big traders realized that they were being monitored and found ways to disguise their actions. The smart trader had to find a new repeater.

Ways to make money with repeaters have included such approaches as repeating price swings, recurring angles, price patterns, and wave count, to name only a few. The basic theory behind Action-Reaction is: what price does in action should repeat in its reaction (see Figure 1). The same process continues where action-reaction techniques are concerned. There are constantly new ways of using this, with traders trying to get the edge on each other by devising new or better uses of this theory. Only a certain amount of basic theory exists, but this may be used in many different combinations.

There are times when the market treads out patterns that repeat themselves for as long as six months on the daily price charts (see Figure 2). At other times no pattern may be found. To find these repetitious price patterns learn how to use "pivot-finder lines." Once a pattern begins to form in a recognizable manner, it can be expected to repeat enough to make money. These patterns are found by repetitious angle lines with parallel lines over equal distances. By learning to use these repetitious angle lines, you can discover the key to unlocking many good trades.

THEORY USED IN PIVOT FINDER LINES

1. Recurring angle methods are often part of the Pivot Finder methods, but the PF techniques include more than the recurring angle theory and methods.

2. Action-reaction theory is included in some cases. Isaac Newton and others put this theory into use. It is one of the physical laws of the universe. If one exerts energy, he eventually needs to rest; if he rests, he has more energy. Likewise it is in the market; if power is used to push the market up, eventually there develops an opposing force to push it back down. There may be resting places along the way, but the forces that move the market are like the energy of a man. If price were to go up continually, things would become so expensive no one would be able to buy them. The opposing force to upward movement is the build up of resistance to high price by consumers and users of the merchandise. When price gets too high, people stop using the product and do without or find a substitute. This is what happened to coal in the fifties. People found other means of energy than coal and for many years coal had been out of favor. With the huge increases in oil prices, coal has started to again be used.

3. Cycles are usually included because they may be seen by repetitious lines equal spaces apart. The lines are not drawn for finding cycles, but those who like to use cycles in their analysis will find that the Pivot Finder

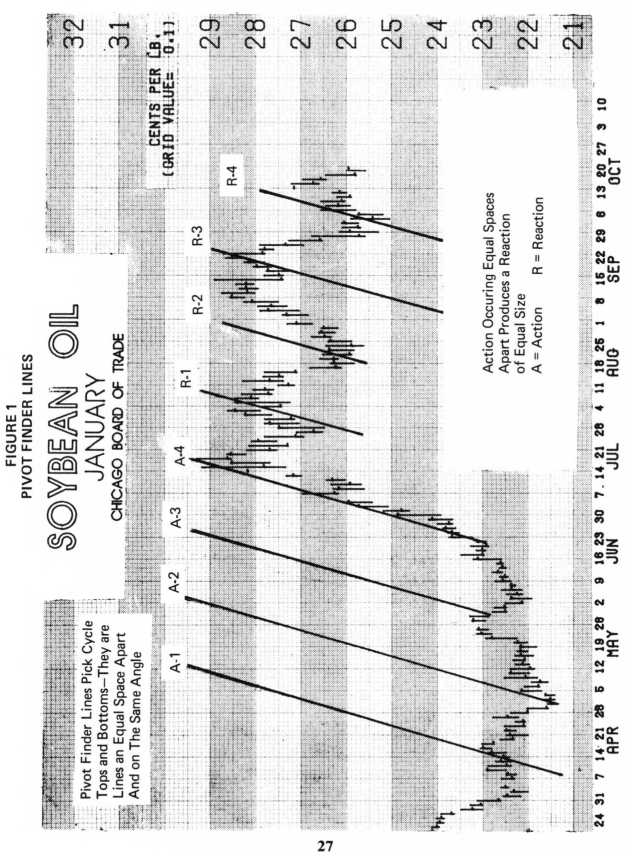

FIGURE 1
PIVOT FINDER LINES

SOYBEAN OIL
JANUARY
CHICAGO BOARD OF TRADE

Pivot Finder Lines Pick Cycle
Tops and Bottoms—They are
Lines an Equal Space Apart
And on The Same Angle

CENTS PER LB.
(GRID VALUE= 0.1)

Action Occuring Equal Spaces
Apart Produces a Reaction
of Equal Size
A = Action   R = Reaction

Chart furnished courtesy Commodity Perspective

27

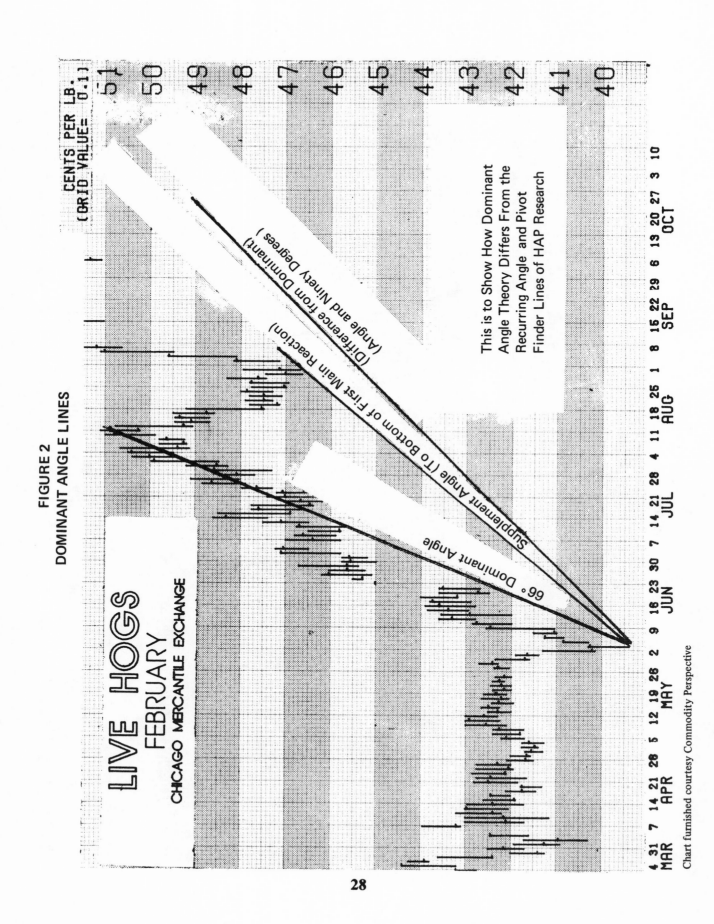

FIGURE 2
DOMINANT ANGLE LINES

LIVE HOGS
FEBRUARY
CHICAGO MERCANTILE EXCHANGE

CENTS PER LB.
(GRID VALUE= 0.1)

This is to Show How Dominant
Angle Theory Differs From the
Recurring Angle and Pivot
Finder Lines of HAP Research

66° Dominant Angle

Supplement Angle (To Bottom of First Main Reaction)
(Difference from Dominant)
(Angle and Ninety Degrees)

Chart furnished courtesy Commodity Perspective

lines make cycle work a lot easier (see Figure 1).

4. Balance Point lines are sometimes the same as a pivot finder line, if parallels are drawn to the balance point line. This is like recurring angle lines; it may be the same at times but the Pivot Finder lines include more and are different most of the time (see Figures 3 and 4).

WHAT OTHERS HAVE DONE IN THIS AREA OF WORK

The author was introduced to angle trading in the early 70's by studying Richard Ney and his dominant angle theory. Since then a number of analysts have written about Ney's methods in their books or magazine articles. Ney used the main peak to low line of a stock as his dominant angle, then he took the difference between this and ninety degrees to find a supplementary angle (see Figure 2). Pivot Finder lines do not necessarily become a peak to low line; and use of the difference between a Pivot Finder line and ninety degrees is not part of this technique.

Channeling by chartists with flop-overs is a beginning in the direction toward Pivot Finder lines, except the chartists are usually only concerned with one channel whereas PFL's are obtained from a study of the entire amount of price action.

W.D. Gann used many angles with parallels. He especially liked the thirty, forty-five, sixty , and ninety degree angles and often drew parallels to them. Other Angle Theory Analysts use methods originated by Gann or make innovations from his methods.

WHAT ARE PIVOT FINDER LINES (PFL)?

Pivot finder lines are parallels, an equal distance apart, that hit on turning points of market action. Many people use the simple channel flopover and this may, at times, be the beginning of a Pivot Finder pattern. What most people do not realize is that many turns of the market come equal distances apart; and the flopover technique can be applied to turning points, if the correct method is learned. W.D. Gann advised traders, over thirty-five years ago, to count the days between turns and to count the days in reactions. He was trying to tell traders that they could learn to find

FIGURE 3

BALANCE POINT LINES WITH PARALLELS

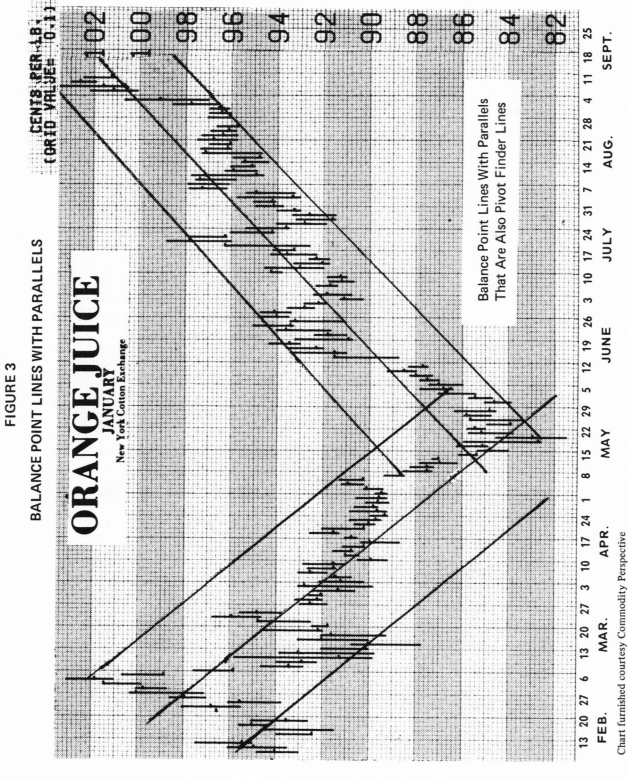

ORANGE JUICE
JANUARY
New York Cotton Exchange

CENTS PER LB.
(GRID VALUE= 0.1)

Balance Point Lines With Parallels
That Are Also Pivot Finder Lines

Chart furnished courtesy Commodity Perspective

30

FIGURE 4

BALANCE POINT LINE

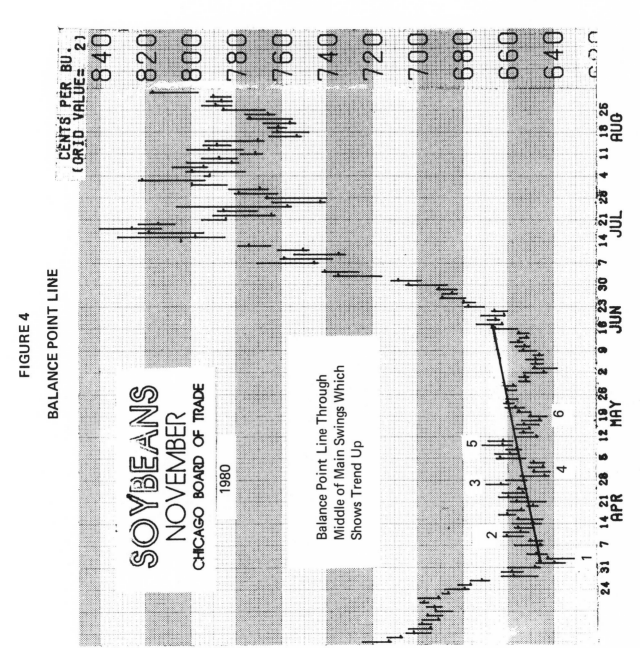

SOYBEANS
NOVEMBER
CHICAGO BOARD OF TRADE

1980

Balance Point Line Through
Middle of Main Swings Which
Shows Trend Up

CENTS PER BU.
(GRID VALUE= 2)

Chart furnished courtesy Commodity Perspective

31

FIGURE 5
RECURRING ANGLE LINES

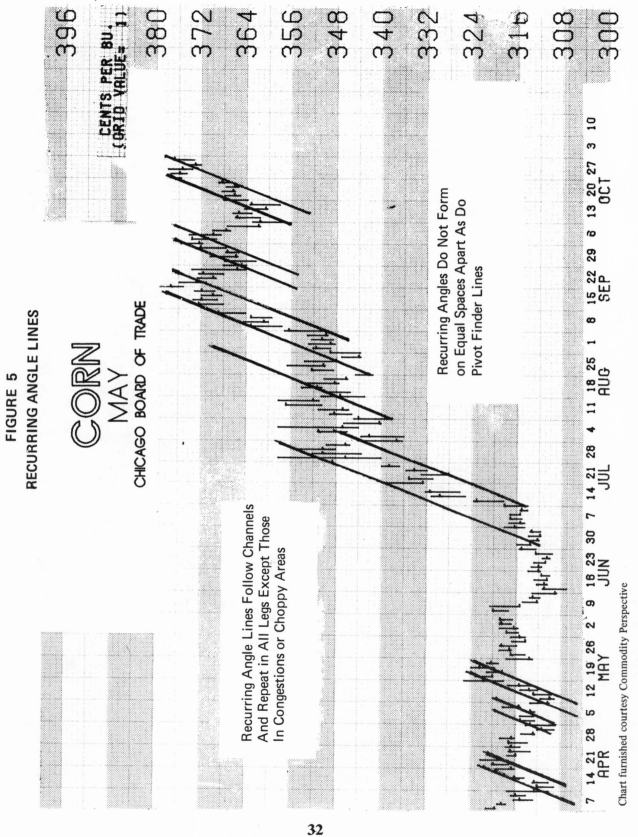

CORN
MAY
CHICAGO BOARD OF TRADE

CENTS PER BU.
(GRID VALUE= 1)

396
380
372
364
356
348
340
332
324
316
308
300

Recurring Angle Lines Follow Channels
And Repeat in All Legs Except Those
In Congestions or Choppy Areas

Recurring Angles Do Not Form
on Equal Spaces Apart As Do
Pivot Finder Lines

7 14 21 28 5 12 19 26 2 9 16 23 30 7 14 21 28 4 11 18 25 1 8 15 22 29 6 13 20 27 3 10
APR   MAY   JUN   JUL   AUG   SEP   OCT

Chart furnished courtesy Commodity Perspective

32

repetitious patterns in the market.

PFL's are lines drawn equal distances out from significant turning points on an angle with the main repetitious angles. See Figure 6 for an example of Pivot Finder lines. Note in the chart how price bounced off the parallel lines out equal distances. Pivots or congestion areas are formed on equal distances. Figure 6 shows that price went back to the last Pivot Finder line, then rolled over to come through the bottom for a good move to the downside. When price failed to make it to the main top line on the third try, this failure resulted in a move in the opposite direction. Here is further proof that it pays to know the days between reactions and swings. It can also be called "a slide-over." As you notice a pattern forming, slide it over expecting repetition. If it does not repeat, this failure indicates what to do. Look for a series of waves like those described by Elliott in his theories of waves patterns.

HOW TO FIND THE PIVOT FINDER LINES

Go back over price charts for about three months or more with drafting tools to find repeating angles and distances between swings or turns. Many times a commodity will travel on the same angle. Also there are times when price will turn each time it comes to a PF line. This may continue for many waves but is usually terminated after five legs of the full span of the movement. There should be three spikes most of the time before a change (see illustrations on Figure 7 and at beginning of angle averaging).

Two main repetitious angle lines should be found, the up and the down. When the lines more vertical are found and drawn on this angle, the lines across should then be found. Note the up lines, down lines and cross line in the illustration on Figure 20. They are like trend lines going out from two pivots. Next measure over the distance of the first sharp reaction and draw a parallel from the turning point. There should be four parallel lines out equal distances apart. Some adjustment may be made as price progresses, but those learning this for the first time are usually amazed at the number of times price will follow these lines or turn when lines are hit.

The rule of alternates should be considered. Out of the three main lines of price action, there can be one which is not even or not of the same length as the others. Usually the alternate form of the pattern will be found in the minor turns leading up to the larger ones.

FIGURE 6
PIVOT FINDER LINES

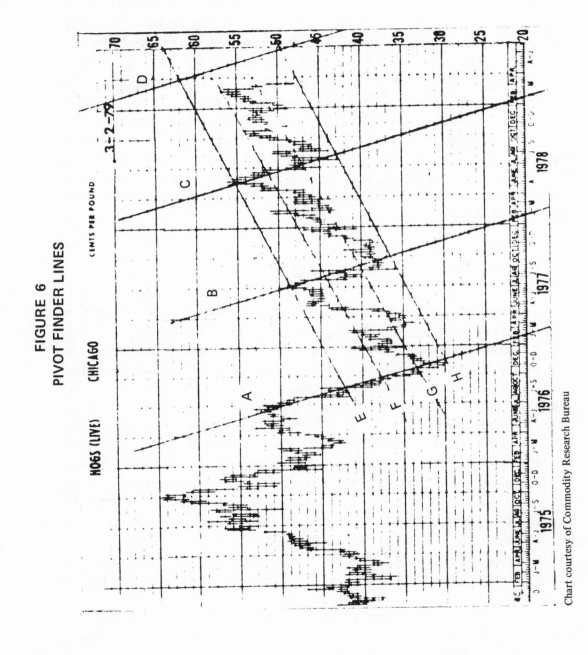

Chart courtesy of Commodity Research Bureau

34

When price fails to travel on the expected angle or one of its parallels, there is usually a process of catching up with choppy sideways congestion area action while price and time balance out. There can be up angle lines, down angle lines, and across angle lines, but usually the across angles are the up angle lines. Look for across lines if there have been very sharp up and down lines.

Some analysts may think that these lines are the same as the 0-3 lines of Action-Reaction taught by Dr. A.H. Andrews, or perhaps the dominant angle lines of Richard Ney; but they are not the same and those who have studied these methods must take care not to mix them. Thousands of charts have been found to yield good Pivot Finder line patterns. If the trader is able to draw channels and find recurring angles, it should not take much practice to see the value of making parallels over an equal distance from these lines, touching the tips of turning points. The orderliness of the universe extends to much of the market if one will learn how to use this information.

The size of the graph is important. Some charting services change the size of their graphs, altering the angles and causing problems. Small charts are not good, and charts with too big a swing will distort the picture. It is best to have charts drawn on a one to one scale.

To help in obtaining the correct angle, it is best to first find the lines on weekly charts. This leaves out a lot of minor swings and gives a longer period of time to search for the right pattern. Some adjustment must be made on price length size when the lines are transferred to the daily charts; but the angles on weeklies and dailies will be about the same if the same scale is used on both. Use the front month of dailies. There will be some difference in the various contracts of the commodity. Just find the recurring angle and use it. The main lines should be on the front month with the largest open interest, and the back month with the largest open interest. Divergence between front months and back months should be noted carefully, to be able to follow the rules of the 3-D technique for interpretation.

Some commodities work easier with these methods than others. It is better to use the markets that have a good following. Some markets are too flat; it is better to work with one having more activity.

When the recurring angles have been found, there is a choice of locating the lines on one side or the other of price action. Before drawing a heavy

35

FIGURE 7
THREE SPIKES

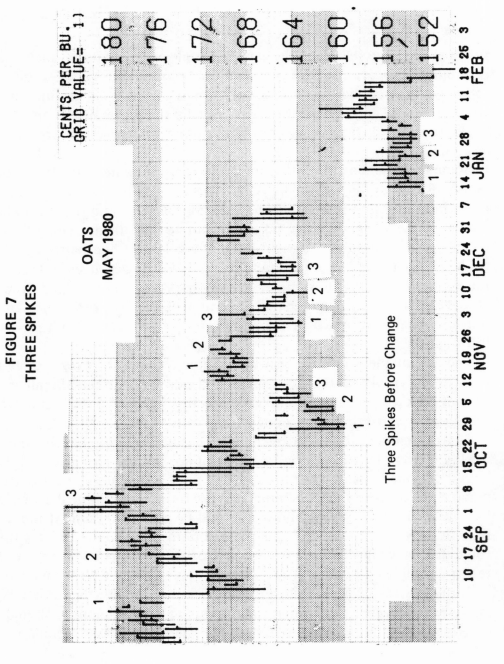

OATS
MAY 1980

Three Spikes Before Change

Chart furnished courtesy Commodity Perspective

36

line, experimentation should be done with transparent material so that the right place for starting is found. This leaves things flexible for alterations as price unfolds when the permanent line is not obvious. Have the lines hitting as many turning points as possible. With practice the layers will stand out and skill will be acquired in finding the main lines of travel of the market action.

GETTING THE LINES RIGHT

Use a parallel ruler; place the first side of the ruler on the temporary line and extend the parallel side out until hitting the price action on the other side (see Figure 8). As the parallel ruler goes out on the same angle across from the main angle temporary line, begin to pick up other swings which have been travelling on this angle. Find the first two swings which conform to the main angle line; then find the distance they are apart and use this on the transparent overlay to get two temporary lines. With both of these temporary lines drawn parallel to each other conforming to the main line of travel, take a scale ruler and place it across these lines in order to see as many turning points as possible. Now note the number on the scale ruler found on each of the temporary lines. The ruler may have to be adjusted several times to get the scale that hits a turning point on a regular basis. Slide the ruler back and forth on this angle to pick up the layers and pivots better. Since the measurements to the temporary lines and the angle are known, there is no fear that the starting place will be lost while sliding the ruler to find the correct distance between the pivot finder lines. Some averaging may be done, or the two lines may be moved slightly to make things work properly, with an even count on most of the equidistant turning points. With practice, getting the distance apart should become easy. All Pivots do not have to be hit, since at least one more set of PFL's will be going in the other direction. What is not found on the down lines will probably be found on the up lines, (or perhaps on the across lines if they are necessary). Try not to make too many lines. This is a common fault of the beginning Angle Analyst.

After finding the main recurring angles and the correct distances apart, draw the lines, extending them out for future price to hit. Some patterns are more difficult than others because of disrupting events like the grain

37

FIGURE 8
PARALLEL RULERS

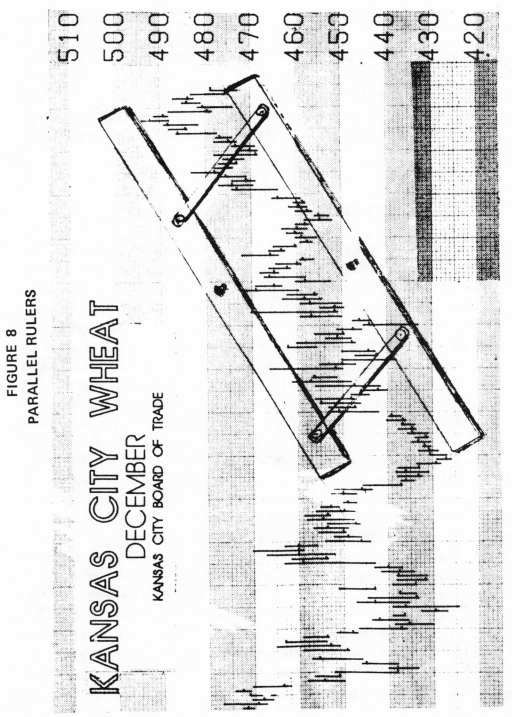

KANSAS CITY WHEAT
DECEMBER
KANSAS CITY BOARD OF TRADE

510
500
490
480
470
460
450
440
430
420

Chart furnished courtesy Commodity Perspective

38

embargo, which threw the natural process of the market temporarily out of balance.

When using charts that have holes or spaces left for holidays, make allowance of about fifteen points, or one-quarter on grains. It is better to have paper drawn on exact scale with scientific precision. If possible draw the line to .001 of an inch on charts with this same precision. In scaling, one day to ten points is all right in meats, but one day to fifteen points will not work. Lines scaled on even numbers for one side should be drawn on even numbers for the opposite set of lines. It should be possible to start on one side of a graph, then draw the lines extending out to intersect price. Be sure that price pays attention to the lines on the daily updates. Divide the layers and waves of price action and identify channels and rhythm of the market. Price will move from one channel to another. Things that would not otherwise be discernable are now seen for better interpretation.

The line going across is usually the one to find the resistance and support areas. The repetitious angle lines are usually the ones being followed by price. The dividing number used should harmonize with the price count by ticks of each market. Since each tick in metals goes ten points, this must be considered in drawing the lines if they are to come out right. A commodity moving on uneven numbers in the market will not come out properly if even numbers are used in drawing the lines. This is especially true of lines going across that must hit the tip of turning points.

The up lines are usually the easiest to find. Working from them, the others will be seen more easily. The lines must be parallel and an equal distance apart to be Pivot Finder lines. Lines hitting the larger pivot swings are more important than those hitting smaller ones. The larger the size of the swing from which the line originates, the more important it is. The strongest lines are those that go by the tip of a number of turning points—the more the better. Pivots on non-overlapping days are also more important. If there is a wide range thrust above other price action, but closing near the lows (or highs) for the day, this is more significant. This is called a critical day. There seems to be a force field at these lines, if the right angle with the right distance apart is drawn.

MAKE TRANSPARENT OVERLAYS

Once it has been established on the temporary acetate overlay that the lines are valid, then permanent lines should be drawn on several pieces. It is suggested that at least three and perhaps four overlays be made. There should be one for the up lines, one for the down lines, and one for the across lines, if these are being used. (Usually the up line will be flat enough that across lines are not needed.) Then make a transparent overlay with ninety degree angle lines coming off the up and down lines. When price goes into a sideways motion after a leg, the sideways motion can be better detected if a ninety degree angle is used off the main angles. The market usually spends some time going sideways before continuing with the main line of travel. At times like these the other lines may not work as well as a ninety degree line off the main repetitious angle line (see Figures 9-13).

HOW TO MAKE THE TRANSPARENT OVERLAY

It is necessary to have a base from which to work the overlay. It should be a ninety degree angle, inscribed so the overlay may be positioned properly with the horizontal and vertical lines of a chart or graph (see Figure 14). The illustration shows two ninety degree angles, one facing down and the other facing up. Inside the ninety degree angle at "A" are examples of angles coming down and going up from the corner of the angle. These are merely for illustration, as the main recurring angle must be found on back price charts and put into the ninety degree angle according to what is found to be the most repetitious angle for both up and down angle lines. The ninety degree line is shown at the end of each recurring angle line, at "B", which should help find congestion areas in price patterns not staying in the channel of the recurring angle. If this ninety degree angle does not suffice in getting the proper lines across the graph, then two more overlays must be made, giving the proper across angle lines at the end of the recurring angle.

If three of these are made, they can be moved apart to make channels on equal distances. (In 1978, we obtained a copyright on these transparent overlays). If need be, extra lines may be put on the overlays. These may be put into position and fastened so they can be used over and over again for the life of a contract. When moving forward to a more distant option, it is easy to unsnap the overlays for minor adjustments needed to have the combinations correct again.

FIGURE 9

PF LINE CONSTRUCTION   #1

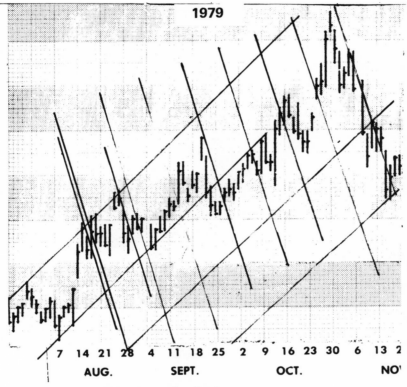

COMMODITY PERSPECTIVE • 327 S. LaSalle • Chicago, Illinois 60604

SOYBEANS
MAY
Chicago Board of Trade

1979

7 14 21 28   4 11 18 25   2 9 16 23 30   6 13 2

AUG.   SEPT.   OCT.   NO'

Chart furnished courtesy Commodity Perspective

Note in beginning, there is only a channel. The flop-over found a congestion.
Then its second extension hit a turn (only known to be temporary for now).

41

FIGURE 10
PF LINE CONSTRUCTION #2

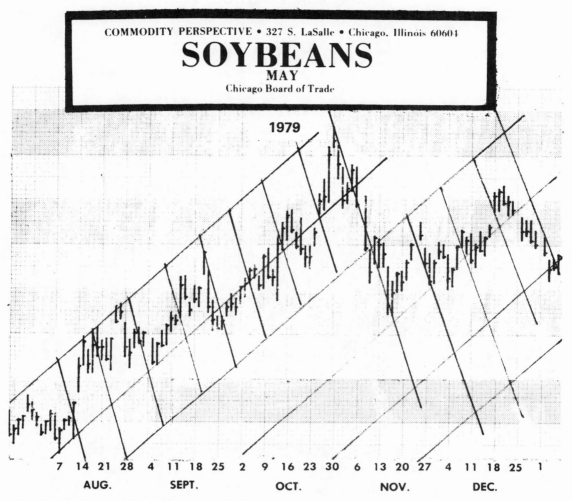

COMMODITY PERSPECTIVE • 327 S. LaSalle • Chicago, Illinois 60604
SOYBEANS
MAY
Chicago Board of Trade

1979

7 14 21 28   4 11 18 25   2 9 16 23 30   6 13 20 27   4 11 18 25 1

AUG.   SEPT.   OCT.   NOV.   DEC.

Chart furnished courtesy Commodity Perspective

These same angles spaced by a beginning channel still give help in finding
Pivots three months beyond its beginning.

The angles and distances apart are known

FIGURE 11
PF LINE CONSTRUCTION #3

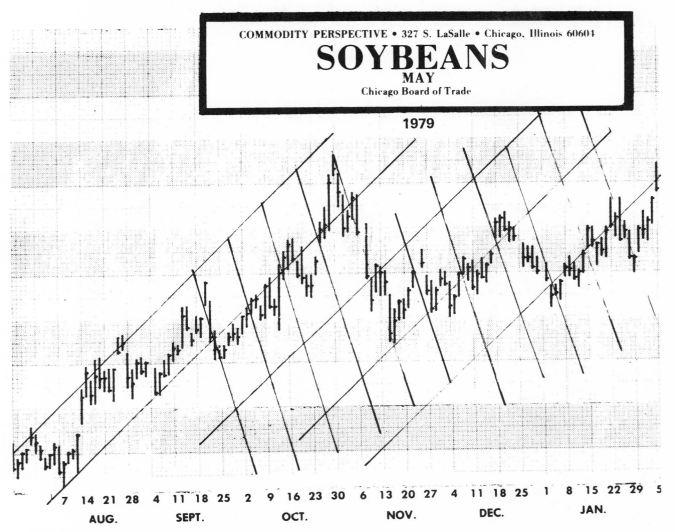

COMMODITY PERSPECTIVE • 327 S. LaSalle • Chicago, Illinois 60604
SOYBEANS
MAY
Chicago Board of Trade

1979

7 14 21 28   4 11 18 25   2 9 16 23 30   6 13 20 27   4 11 18 25   1 8 15 22 29 5

AUG.   SEPT.   OCT.   NOV.   DEC.   JAN.

Chart furnished courtesy Commodity Perspective

Here the lines are still giving help. It is seen that most of the middle lines
can be omitted.

43

FIGURE 12
PF LINE CONSTRUCTION #4

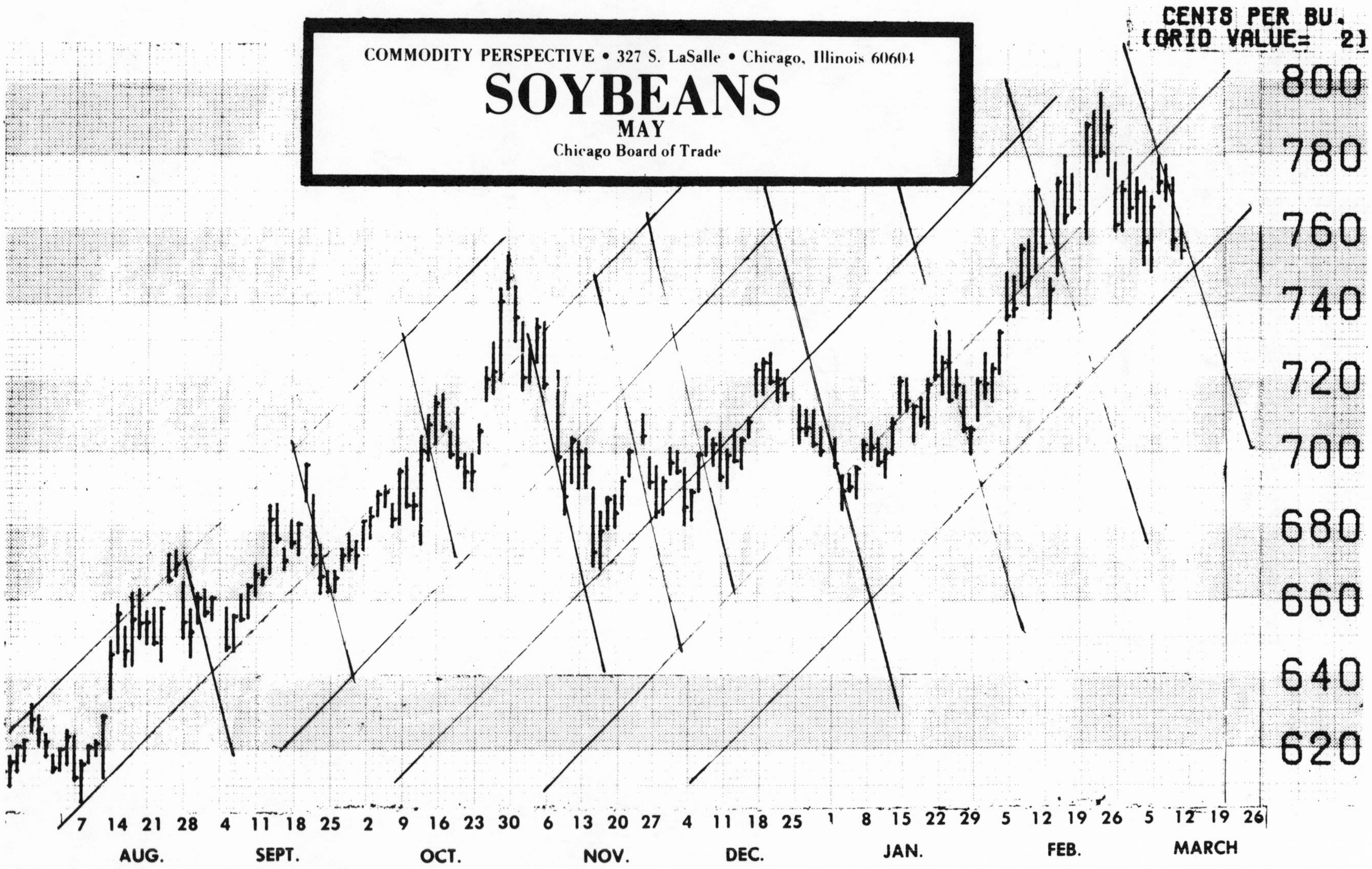

CENTS PER BU.
(GRID VALUE= 2)

800 780 760 740 720 700 680 660 640 620

COMMODITY PERSPECTIVE • 327 S. LaSalle • Chicago, Illinois 60604

SOYBEANS
MAY
Chicago Board of Trade

7 14 21 28 4 11 18 25 2 9 16 23 30 6 13 20 27 4 11 18 25 1 8 15 22 29 5 12 19 26 5 12 19 26

AUG. SEPT. OCT. NOV. DEC. JAN. FEB. MARCH

Chart furnished courtesy Commodity Perspective

Here is the result of extending angles and distances—a part of a channel starting August 1978 going to March 1979.

FIGURE 13
PF LINE CONSTRUCTION #5

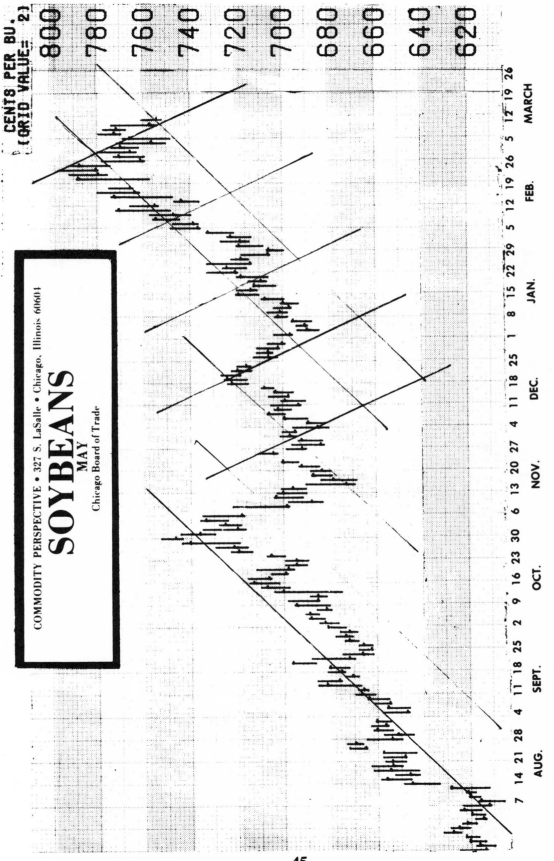

COMMODITY PERSPECTIVE • 327 S. LaSalle • Chicago, Illinois 60601

SOYBEANS
MAY
Chicago Board of Trade

CENTS PER BU.
(GRID VALUE = 2)

Chart furnished courtesy Commodity Perspective

Here the channels have been moved to conform to the slippage started September 25th.
This channel found remaining channels better.

45

FIGURE 14

TOES EXAMPLE

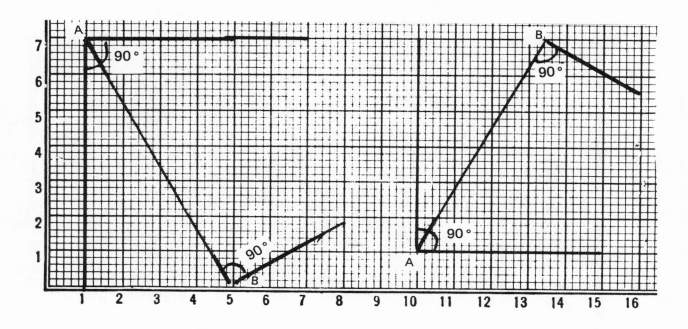

46

INSTRUCTION FOR USE OF THE PIVOT FINDER OVERLAY

1. Align the Pivot Finder overlay so that price is caught between the lines in a channel. The lines should catch the layers and waves.

2. Have as many turning points as is possible on the lines, or coming at the tops or bottoms. You should find that about 80% of the turning points come within twenty points of a line.

3. Closing prices are considered more important.

4. When the Pivot Finder overlay is aligned properly, staple it down on one side, leaving the other side free to add lines or update the price.

5. Count the lines from one turning point to the next and expect the same number on the other side.

6. Determine what Elliott Wave count the market is in. The last leg of a move should end in both an "O" and TP 5 count of the Elliott Wave.

7. Use all lines that intersect three pivots. (Count gaps as a pivot).

HOW TO USE PIVOT FINDER LINES

Pivot Finder lines are an extra tool, to be used like the recurring angle lines and the balance point lines. Regular channel rules apply here. Sell signals occur when price turns down from the top, and buy signals when price bounces off the bottom line and starts up. These lines make it much easier to count the days or space between reactions and to note when contractions or expansions occur.

Elliott wave count should be put on the lines. Note example of July Corn (Figure 15) where this has been done. Other important lines may also be drawn on the overlay. Use a felt pen that will erase easily when the line is not needed. Note on the July Sugar chart (Figure 20) that lines are drawn from a pivot intersecting the middle of the next swing and extending on out to hit price. These are median lines, as taught by Dr. A.H. Andrews in his Action-Reaction course. We will explain these in more detail in Chapter 5, "The Median Line Method."

47

SUMMARY OF USE FOR PIVOT FINDER LINES

1. Slideovers of channels
2. Framework for Elliott use
3. Help with cycles and time price balancing
4. An extra indicator as price bounces off a line
5. Use of the mid-swing technique

The Mid-Swing line is a reverse median line. It comes from the middle of a swing under the bottom of the next swing in an up market, or over the top of the next swing in a down market. See illustration below:

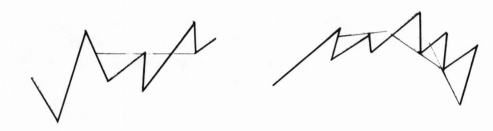

Note that until the midline swing is broken, the trader stays in the market. This can only be used on zig-zag type price patterns, however.

6. Important lines must be included with the Pivot Finder lines. Any line passing through the tips of three or more pivots is important. Here gaps are counted the same as pivots, so lines that go through them qualify as PF lines. To keep from overlooking important lines, one should take a transparent ruler and gradually move it around the chart in a complete sweep, noting the times three or more pivots are tipped at once, then drawing different colored lines here.

7. Any time two or more lines meet at the same place with price, consider this much more important (see Figure 16).

TRADING STRATEGY

1. Buy or sell when price comes into intersection with two or more PF lines.
2. Trade primarily with major trend.
3. Watch the Elliott wave count for P5 areas.
4. Take one-half of price from one main channel to the next.

FIGURE 15

ELLIOTT COUNT ON PIVOT LINES

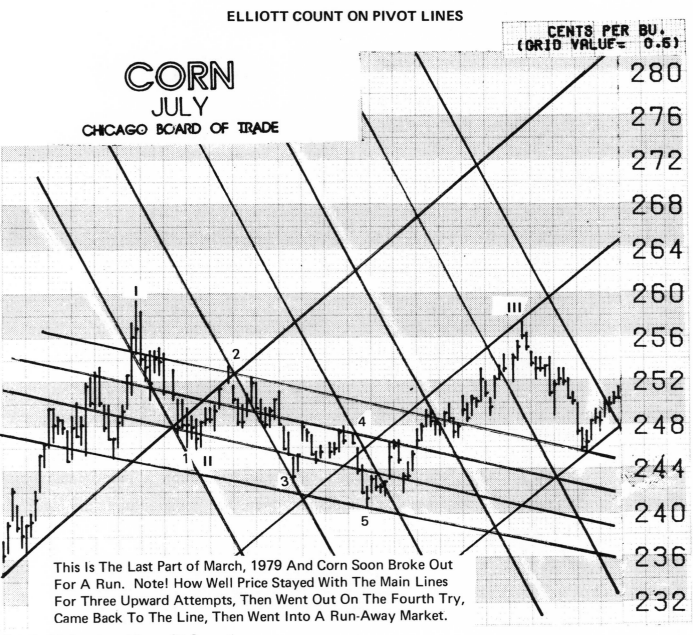

This Is The Last Part of March, 1979 And Corn Soon Broke Out
For A Run. Note! How Well Price Stayed With The Main Lines
For Three Upward Attempts, Then Went Out On The Fourth Try,
Came Back To The Line, Then Went Into A Run-Away Market.

Chart furnished courtesy of Commodity Perspective

FIGURE 16

THREE TWO PIVOT LINES

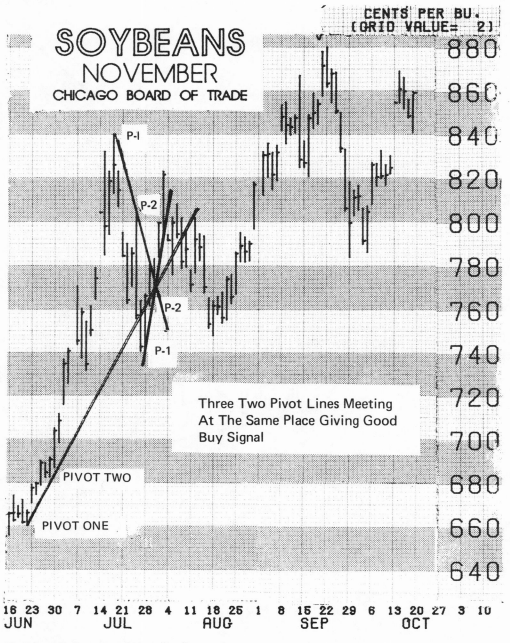

Three Two Pivot Lines Meeting At The Same Place Giving Good Buy Signal

Chart furnished courtesy Commodity Perspective

FIGURE 17

THREE PIVOT LINES

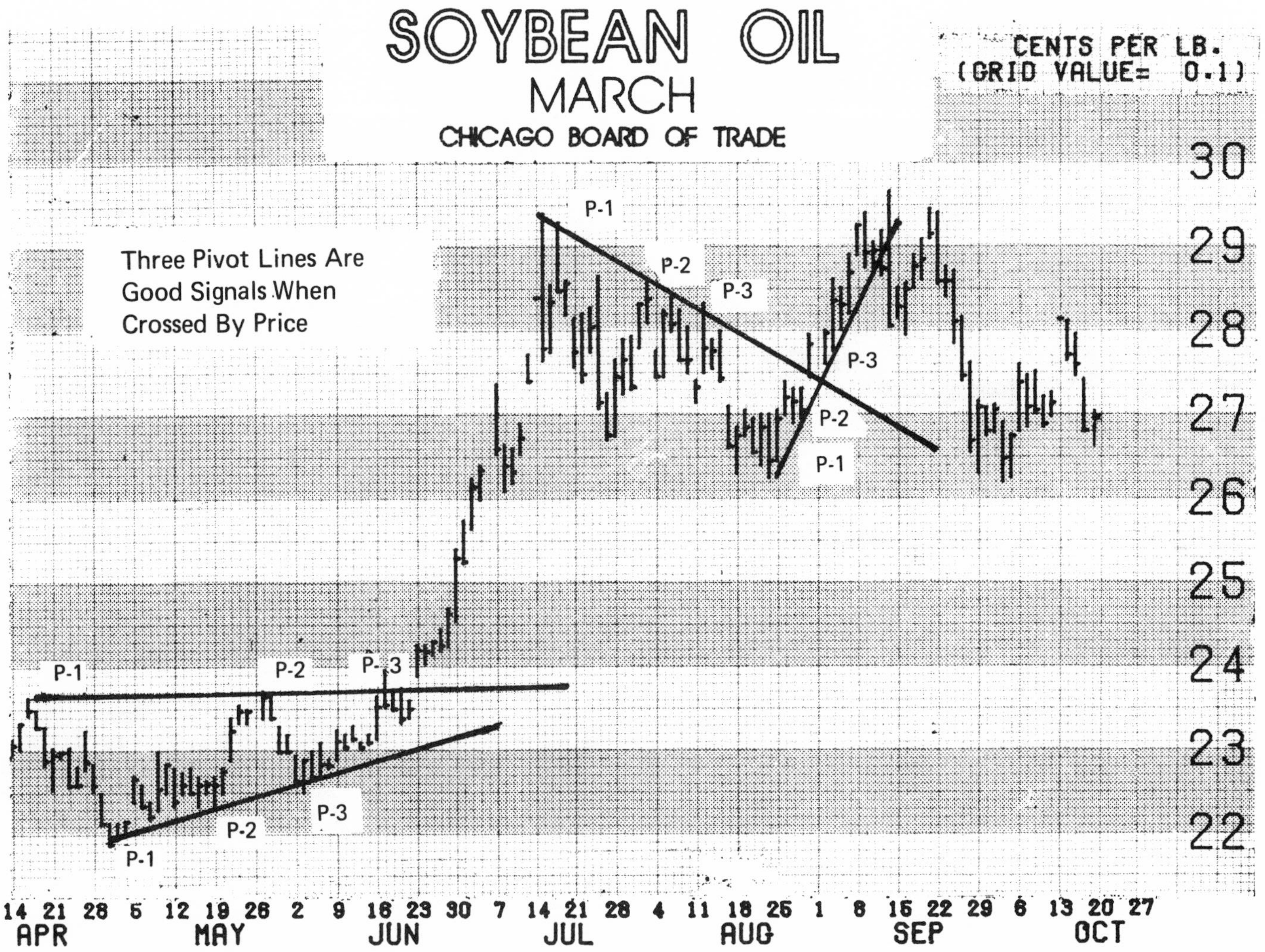
SOYBEAN OIL
MARCH
CHICAGO BOARD OF TRADE
CENTS PER LB.
(GRID VALUE= 0.1)
Three Pivot Lines Are Good Signals When Crossed By Price
P-1
P-2
P-3
P-1
P-2
P-3
P-1
P-2
P-3
P-1
P-2
P-3
30
29
28
27
26
25
24
23
22
14 21 28 5 12 19 26 2 9 16 23 30 7 14 21 28 4 11 18 25 1 8 15 22 29 6 13 20 27
APR
MAY
JUN
JUL
AUG
SEP
OCT

Chart furnished courtesy of Commodity Perspective

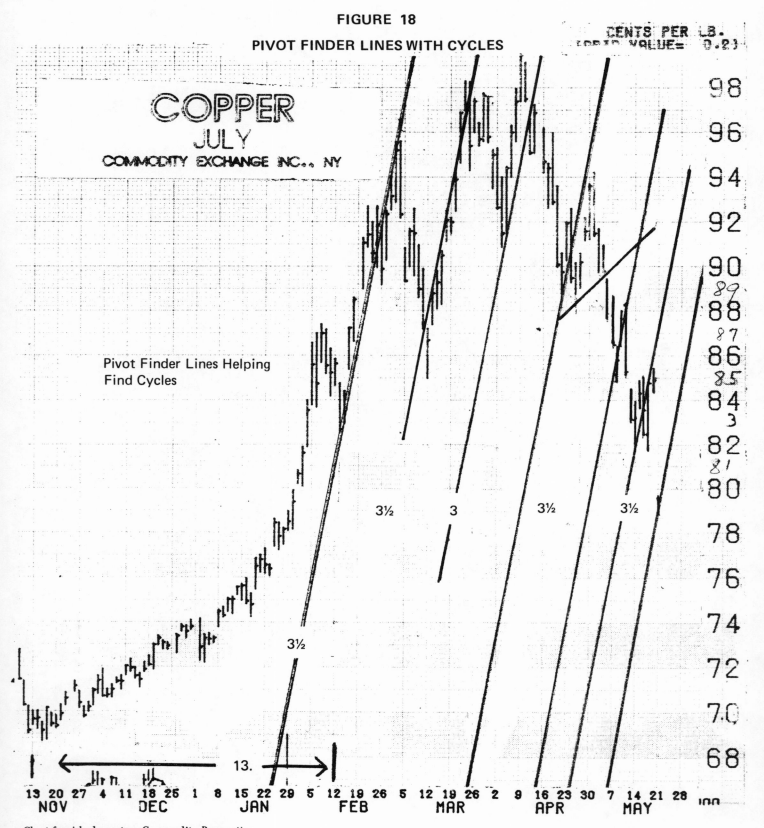

FIGURE 18

PIVOT FINDER LINES WITH CYCLES

COPPER
JULY
COMMODITY EXCHANGE INC., NY

Pivot Finder Lines Helping
Find Cycles

Chart furnished courtesy Commodity Perspective

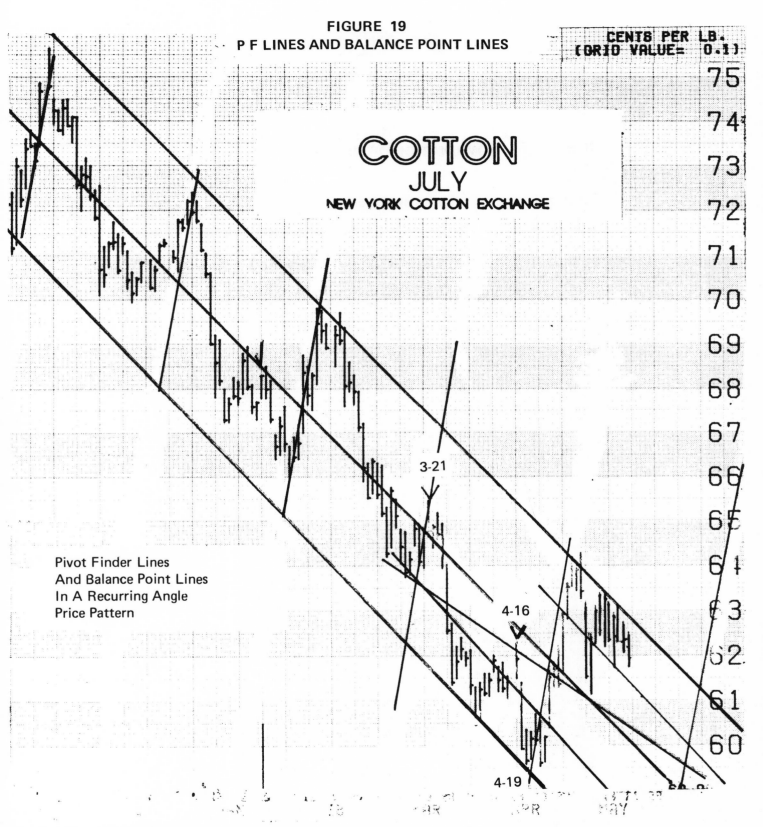

FIGURE 19
P F LINES AND BALANCE POINT LINES

CENTS PER LB.
(GRID VALUE= 0.1)

COTTON
JULY
NEW YORK COTTON EXCHANGE

Pivot Finder Lines
And Balance Point Lines
In A Recurring Angle
Price Pattern

3-21

4-16

4-19

Chart furnished courtesy of Commodity Perspective

53

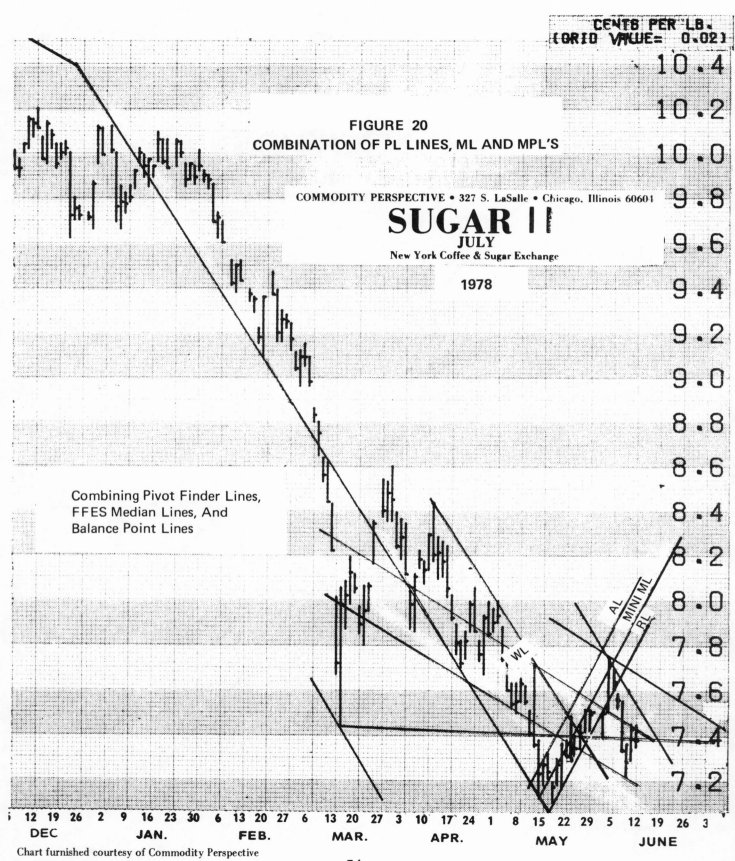

FIGURE 20
COMBINATION OF PL LINES, ML AND MPL'S

COMMODITY PERSPECTIVE • 327 S. LaSalle • Chicago, Illinois 60604

SUGAR II

JULY
New York Coffee & Sugar Exchange

1978

Combining Pivot Finder Lines,
FFES Median Lines, And
Balance Point Lines

CENTS PER LB.
(GRID VALUE= 0.02)

FIGURE 21

P F LINES

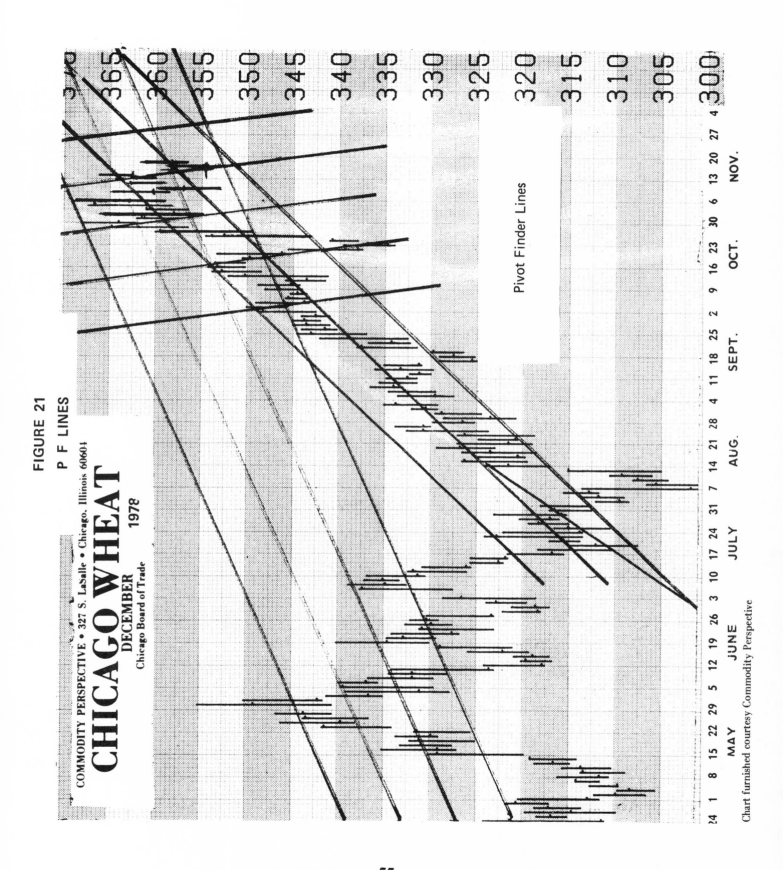

COMMODITY PERSPECTIVE • 327 S. LaSalle • Chicago, Illinois 60604

CHICAGO WHEAT
DECEMBER 1978
Chicago Board of Trade

Pivot Finder Lines

Chart furnished courtesy Commodity Perspective

55

CHAPTER 3

WIDGETS AND TOES

WHAT ARE WIDGETS AND TOES?

Interpretive lines put on transparent overlays are sometimes called "Widgets." This name was first used by students of Ralph Dystant to describe his calculator. Similar things have been used for many years by Gann followers, to help with his geometric lines. Toes are transparent overlays, or just another kind of widget.

WHAT THE WIDGETS DO

When repetitious lines are needed to help interpret markets, the widgets work better than drawing lines on several charts. Angles needed from a peak to low line can be seen in relation with the price action beneath them without cluttering a page. Different types of overlays may be applied to the same price action for better interpretation. These can be like a gauge or a speedometer for a car, giving the velocity and time-price relationships.

TYPES OF WIDGET LINES

1. Momentum recognition from angle of travel
2. Time and price balancing
3. Fibonacci ratio lines drawn to scale with the charts
4. Speedlines
5. Trendlines and channels
6. Harmonics

KINDS OF WIDGETS

1. Those of Ralph Dystant. Old copies and use of these may be seen by way of the Davis Book Service of Wayzata, Minnesota. They are hard to locate and probably obsolete; but those found give an idea of use and concept.

It is an overlay with angles from a base line, obviously a takeoff from the calculators of W.D. Gann. Its use and value depends upon special knowledge and understanding. Since the material we saw was old, and we do not wish to violate proprietary boundaries, we will not try to explain how it works. Below is an illustration:

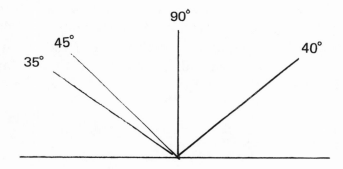

2. HAP Widgets or Overlays.

a. The Conwidge has a base line with thirty, forty-five and sixty degree angle lines off of the base. Lay the base line on a peak to low line, with the converging line point "o" at the pivot. This has been illustrated in the Square of a Circle Chart, Figure 19 of my previous book, *Advanced Commodity Trading Techniques.*

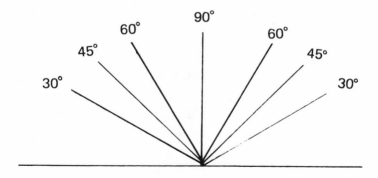

The thirty and sixty degree lines should be helpful in finding resistance or support areas, while the forty-five degree line is a balancing line showing the progress of price in relation with time. These lines often find turns of the market.

b. The Fibwidge has lines on Fib ratios around a base line. With this, the Fibonacci time-price area can be quickly recorded for use. This is illustrated in *Advanced Commodity Trading Techniques,* Figure 18.

c. The Tenwidge is an all purpose or catch-all type. It is used by FFES Action Reaction, with the lines coming down from a high as well as up from a low on ten degree angles. These are aligned to hit on a significant pivot, with the other lines in position to be intercepted by price action (see Figure 22). These widgets allow a number of indicators to be used on a chart without drawing lines.

3. West's Widget

James J. West has a widget that is amazing. It is a combination of Fibonacci ratios with harmonic lines. Evidently the person constructing this studied under Ralph Dystant, since it shows his handiwork so strongly. The widget, illustrated below, is most complex.

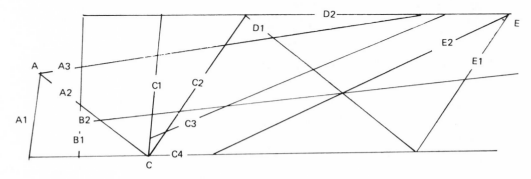

59

WORKING THE WIDGETS

1. West's Widget

When this is placed upon Commodity Perspective charts, such as the pork bellies, it will go off tops to find the lows; or off lows to find the highs. When placing its middle angle point "c" on a pivot, it often finds the end of this move on out-going angle lines.

The "A" point and "A-1" line can be a starting place. Put the point on a pivot and let the line go out to another pivot. This line may need extending further than is shown in the illustration. With the A-1 line parallel with two pivots, note the B-2 line and C-3 line.

The B point and B-1 line may be also used for alignment. Note especially the C-2, C-3, and C-4 lines (see Figures 23 and 24 for examples).

HAP'S WIDGETS USE

These are to be used anywhere they are needed in place of drawing lines. They are handy gadgets to use to find congestion areas or turning points. The point is to save time and to be able to do more with a chart before it is ruined by drawing many different lines on it.

WAYS TO USE THE WIDGETS

1. For estimating the percentage of price progress: 5, 10, 15, 20% lines.
2. For evaluating time and price relationships.
3. For obtaining quickly the square of a number.
4. For Fibonacci number location.
5. For cycle time period location.
6. For revealing repetitious angles.
7. For momentum angle comparisons.

FIGURE 22

ANGLE LINES

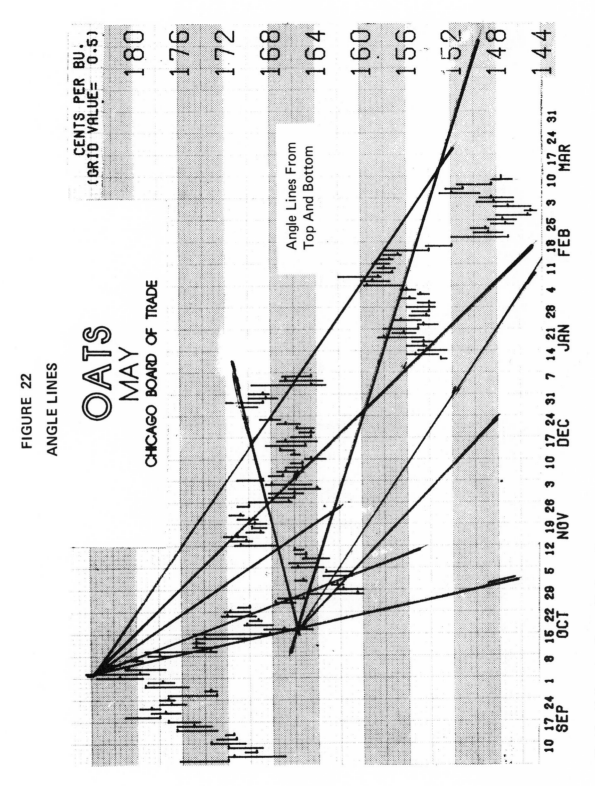

OATS
MAY
CHICAGO BOARD OF TRADE

CENTS PER BU.
(GRID VALUE= 0.5)

180
176
172
168
164
160
156
152
148
144

Angle Lines From
Top And Bottom

10 17 24   1 8 15 22 29   5 12 19 26   3 10 17 24 31   7 14 21 28   4 11 18 25   3 10 17 24 31
SEP   OCT   NOV   DEC   JAN   FEB   MAR

Chart furnished courtesy Commodity Perspective

61

FIGURE 23
WEST'S WIDGET #1

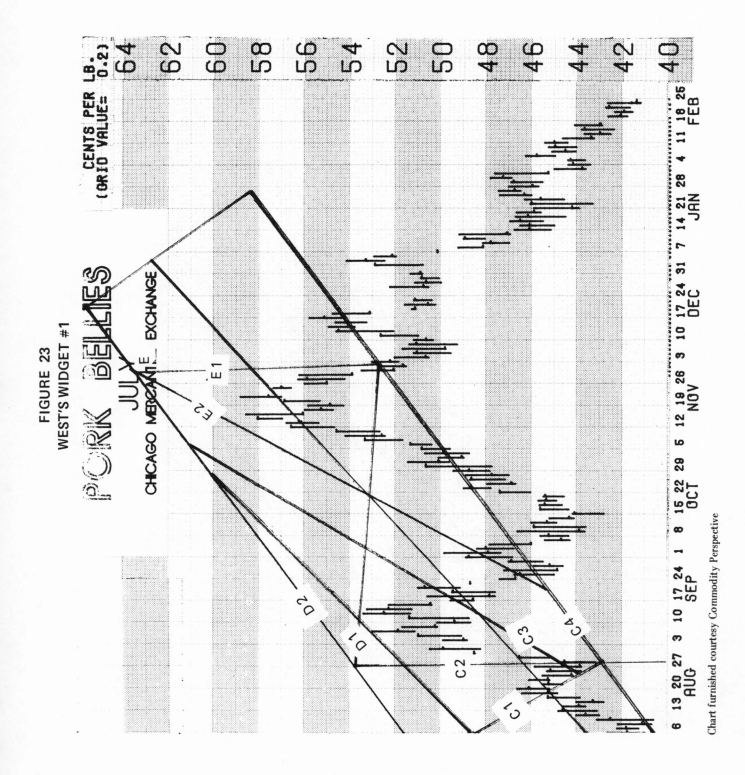

Chart furnished courtesy Commodity Perspective

62

FIGURE 24
WEST'S WIDGET #2

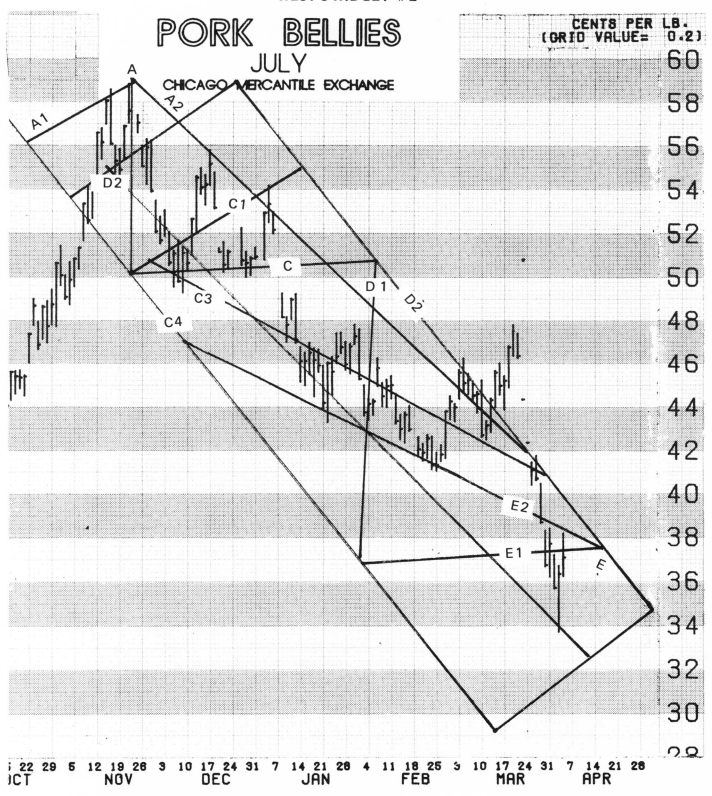

PORK BELLIES
JULY
CHICAGO MERCANTILE EXCHANGE

CENTS PER LB.
(GRID VALUE= 0.2)

Chart furnished courtesy Commodity Perspective

63

VALUE OF THE WIDGETS

Keeping neat charts is important. Having to draw several charts is time consuming and can be avoided with use of the widgets. Different kinds of overlays may be used when they seem appropriate, but may be kept out of the way when others are needed. These will help reveal more plainly the time and price relationships necessary for making analysis.

These widgets may be made with any combination desired. An interesting variation is to have recurring angles as base lines, then put forty, sixty-five, ninety, one hundred-five, and one hundred forty-four degree angles out from the base lines. This combines the recurring angles with Fib numbers (based on fives and ones). The ninety should be 89 for a Fib number, but is close enough , and by using the ninety, the charts can be kept square with the widget. The ninety is also needed with the recurring angles.

FIGURE 25
HAP WIDGET

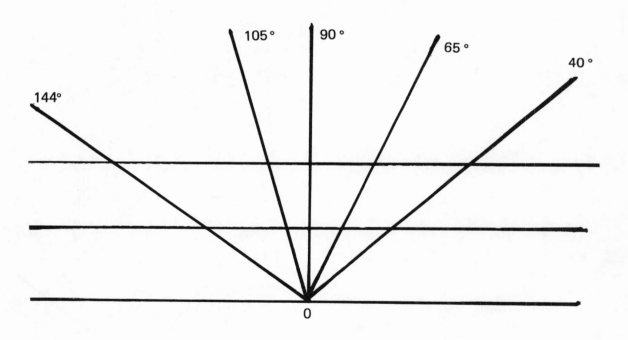

FIGURE 26
COMP WIDGES

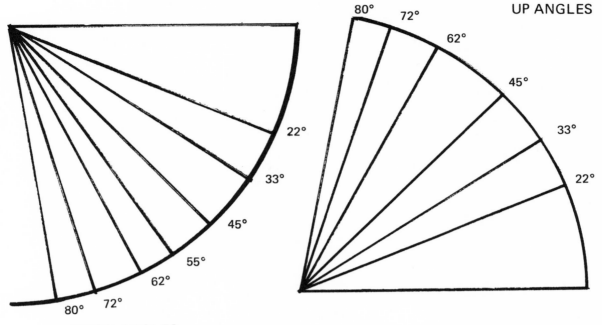

UP ANGLES

80° 72° 62° 45° 33° 22°

22° 33° 45° 55° 62° 72° 80°

DOWN ANGLES

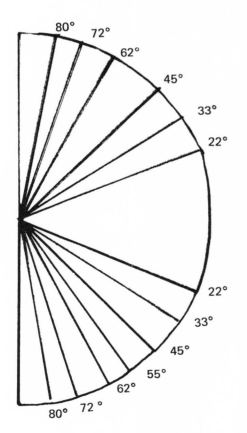

80° 72° 62° 45° 33° 22°

22° 33° 45° 55° 62° 72° 80°

Comparison Angles For A Quick
Check On The Strength Or
Weakness Of A Market

Velocity And Momentum
May Be Seen Quickly Too,·
By Using These Widgets

CHART SCALE

65

CHAPTER 4

ACCUMULATION DISTRIBUTION METHODS

STAYING OUT OF TROUBLE

Many traders have a good trading plan with some excellent trading techniques, but give up a lot of their profits by not knowing when to get out; or by getting into trouble with what would have been a good trade. These traders have been exhorted on the importance of taking a position and staying with it. They are heeding good advice, but often find a trade that once had good profits has become a loss. They bemoan the gains lost and wonder if they can stay in to make it back again.

There are many long term trading plans without a proper method of indicating when conditions have changed. There should be a way to know when the smart money is moving in, or getting out.

THE PART THAT REALLY COUNTS

Short term traders are not too concerned with this type of problem, since they are going with the swings, trying to pick up a few points. Intermediate traders need to give this some concern. It is especially important to the position trader who attempts to get in at the beginning of a move and stay with it. Many big winners say the only way to make it is to keep holding on in the manner of Cutten, who became famous for successful long term trading.

The first fact a long term trader must realize is that most price action in the market is not relevant to the longer term trends. To look at this move closely, think about the percentage of traders who trade for the long pull. There are many more floor scalpers and short term traders. Then there are those who change their minds, get sick, or have personal problems. Some will be taking short swing profits while others decide to go on vacation. It has been estimated by some good market analysts that 75% of the market action is not pertinent. To be conservative, we will say that 70% is not applicable to long term trading.

WHY ONLY PART OF MARKET ACTION IS IMPORTANT FOR LONG TERM TRADES

There are approximately twelve possible ways for a person to be in a trade. These can be summarized as those who think wrong and admit it, those who are right and not proven wrong, those who are in and do not want to change, and those who are forced to change. Now those who put on a bad trade can do one of five things: reverse; get out; hedge; get out but come back later in the day; or wait and wonder what to do. Those who are right have four possibilities: stay in; spread; test the market to prove they are right; or wait and hope they keep doing okay. The first two of the twelve really do not count, because if someone is forced out he is not apt to be coming back soon and those who have a good position do not want to change.

They may be right and not know it, or wrong and not know it. All kinds of rumors and scare tactics are spread out to traders. Even high ranking officials are sometimes maneuvered into doing things that will drastically affect the market. It makes better headline news to print scare stories about the weather. Traders are constantly being buffeted by events or stories that may shake their position or may cause them to go into a bad position. Some people even trade by astrological signs because they think radiation from planets affects the market psychology.

As we saw above, there are twelve possibilities, but two of these do not count. Regarding the ten left, a number of reasons can be given to prove that most of these will not stay in the market very long. The person who really proves that he will stick is the one who reverses his position if he thinks he is wrong.

68

Further evidence may be seen in point and figure charting. Note on most of these charts, using intra-day price action, that about seventy percent of trading is in some congestion. Long term traders only trade when they think price will go out of the congestion area. So it seems logical to believe that only thirty percent of market action applies to the longer term trade of three weeks or more in time.

WHAT THIS MEANS TO THE LONG TERM TRADER

By long term trader, we mean someone who wants to do more than trade for three day or four day swings. We are thinking of those who are playing the three week swings, or longer. This is not the usual concept of a long term trader, but we need to distinguish the long term trader and are lumping all others together.

Only thirty percent of price action has bearing on what these longer term traders want to do, and this also applies to volume and open interest. This may be the reason that some traders become careless. It can be easy to slip into an "it doesn't matter" frame of mind. The trader, however, does not know which thirty percent applies to him, or which direction the thirty percent is favoring unless he has some good indicators. It can be that all the thirty percent may be lumped in one day or several days as opposed to a ten-day average. It does seem relevant to assume that a price change of over thirty percent of the ten days price average would apply a lot more to the long term trader.

People already in the market and not wanting to change would not be affecting the rise or fall of present price. It is just the ones currently trading who are forcing the price up or down and who will count; so only a short term average is needed. A ten day average should be sufficient. We assume that those thirty five percent above a ten day MA are buying on a longer term basis; and those thirty five percent below the ten day MA are selling for the longer term. Most of the day trader's activity should be filtered out by the moving average; then the thirty five percent band above and below the moving average is filtering out even more; so it should be safe to assume that the rest is in for the long term.

As an indication of the strongest, the longs or the shorts, one can assume that the number of times price went above the moving average (or below

69

the moving average) and above the thirty percent price filter band indicates which is the strongest.

WHAT THE LONG TERM TRADER NEEDS TO KNOW

The long term trader needs to know who his competitors are. He needs to learn to disregard the small chopping action caused by the short term traders. He knows that only thirty percent of price action applies to him and he needs methods to tell which part of price action to be concerned about. Volume and open interest may help him, but most volume and open interest figures do not apply to his work. This seems like a formidable obstacle to overcome. However, we feel that these questions and problems can be solved.

WHAT OTHERS HAVE DONE TO SOLVE THIS PROBLEM

It is generally considered that the hedgers are in the market for a long trade. It is reported that about 58% of the action is by hedgers. Some people compare the "position of traders report" with open interest. We did work on this in 1978. The percentage of those in large positions can be applied to the open interest and changes noted for each month. The Commodity Research Bureau has been doing this for twenty years, and publishing it in the annual Commodity Yearbook. They have taken ten year averages of what the large traders have done on most commodities, using this means of interpretation. With these they can tell when the present positions are above or below the normal. All traders should see and use this information.

Larry Williams, in his book, *How I Made a Million,* has an accumulation distribution method whereby he judged the amount of change from the opening to the high or low of the day and made a formula to plot on an oscillator. This has been successful and many traders are still using it.

Some traders try to judge the accumulation or distribution by price patterns. It is said that quiet markets near historical lows are accumulation, and hectic swinging markets near historical highs are distribution. This, however, can be deceiving or confusing at times. There may be a swinging or choppy bottom, not a quiet slow one; and at times markets top out by slowly rolling over, or just simply making a "V" turn. Those who rely on the old concept of price patterns would be out of luck in these situations. There are years, like 1977, when commodities just chop around or swing up and down without making much of a move either way.

It would be better if the commitment of large trader percentage for a month be applied to back months of a commodity. It stands to reason that hedgers will be more inclined to go into the back months of a commodity rather than the front months because they will not have to move around so much. If a hedger goes into a front month, he must be rolling forward on a regular basis. If there is an inverted market, with the front months higher than the back, this would be profitable; but most long term traders do not want to be changing positions, so they go into a back month. The short term traders use the front months more. So using the back months here will help make the percentages better with this indicator.

The 3-D method of judging the strength of a front month against a back month will help show what the big traders are doing in comparison to the little ones (see Figure 27).

W.D. Gann instructed his followers to do three-day swing charting. This method eliminated the changes that were less than three days and took a lot of the minor movement out of the market. See the chart illustrating this, Figure 28.

Moving averages take the minor swings out of a market and help traders just as well as the use of weeklies or monthlies, which take out minor moves. Long term traders should trade primarily from weekly charts.

Charles Drummond has published his P & L charting method, which averages out the price of three days to filter minor moves from the market.

WHAT IS VITAL

Looking at what we have found, it can be seen that most price action does not apply to long term traders. If we apply this to price, we know that there needs to be a change out of a flat channel (or narrow price range) before it applies since we are going by averages. Open interest may or

OHAMA 3-D ANALYTICAL TECHNIQUE

Most commodity analytical techniques involve two dimensions — time and the various parameters of the given commodity such as price, open interest, volume, etc. The Ohama technique adds a vital new third dimension (the significance of the 3-D) to analysis, i.e., the various contract months of a given commodity and their interrelationships.

This analytical technique developed by William Ohama is a new and powerful means of identifying intermediate and major tops and bottoms by detecting when the market principals accumulate or distribute a significant number of contracts. The market principals are the major producers, distributors such as the huge grain and cotton holding companies, and the processors. These principals are generally acknowledged the best fundamentalists in the commodity business, and rightfully so, since they have the largest stake in the market. It is therefore extremely important for them to properly hedge and spread. Consequently the principals spend huge sums of money researching every aspect of the particular commodity or commodities involved in their business. Further, when the principals require loans, their bankers usually insist that the principals hedge in the futures market as a condition for granting the loans.

Normally the principals are in the commodity market to hedge. To hedge, the producers are short, the processors are long, and the distributors are long, short or spread depending upon their commitments to the producers and the processors.

However, any of the principals may also spread if the market goes against them or spread to lock in profits achieved by prior market action. It is this continuous interplay by the principals of cash buying, selling, hedging, and spreading which usually determines the course of the market.

Through their intimate knowledge of the market, the principals are often able to identify intermediate and major tops and bottoms at which point they initiate or liquidate positions.

For example — the activity by the principals is indicated when one contract month does not make a new high when the other contracts months do. Heavy shorting by the principals in this one month prevents the price from rising to new highs as it is in other months. The reverse applies for bottoms.

A price reversal without reaching a new high or low (as the case may be) accompanied by high volume in just one contract month is a key indicator. Also, the principals are usually more active in the market when a trend line is crossed or when all contract months are making new highs or lows.

The Open Interest and Volume action in the various contract months can usually be used to confirm an Ohama 3-D.

The accompanying charts illustrate the principle employed in the Ohama 3-D technique.

To facilitate the use of the Ohama 3-D technique, *all* contract months for each commodity are charted and available. However, when a 3-D occurs, it usually can be detected by reviewing only those charts covering the contract months having the major portion of the Open Interest. Hence for a given commodity, a set of charts is offered as an item of the service. The number of charts in a set ranges from 3 to 5 charts, depending upon the commodity.

FIGURE 27
OHAMA 3-D TECHNIQUE

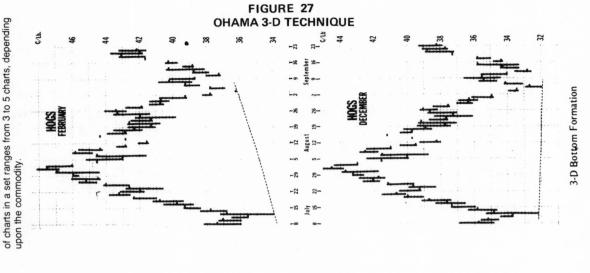

3-D Bottom Formation

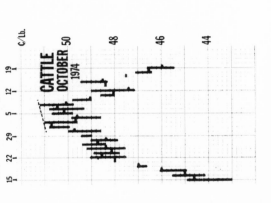

3-D Top Formation

72

may not already have the long term traders in the market. Volume does not seem to be much help unless there is at least a 30% over MA increase for several days. The commitment of traders reports, as used by the Commodity Research Bureau, seem to have a lot of merit and should help.

THE KIND OF MARKETS INVOLVED

Most people think that accumulation or distribution takes place in congestion areas or choppy markets. Stop and think about this! Who is taking the opposite side when the market breaks out and starts running with twice the normal acceleration? Could it be the people who took a position down on the bottom deciding that they will take some profits? Little traders certainly do not ordinarily have the nerve to buck a runaway market. It must be well funded people. Who has the money to go against a run with large losses before the tide turns and profits are made? It is the large trader with big money, or the hedger who is locking in a profit against his cash crop or product. The short-term traders and little traders are trying to scalp a profit out of the running market. It is the profit taker or the hedger who is taking the opposite side in this market. The smart trader has accumulated on the bottom and takes profits when the market begins to run.

Now comes the first congestion area period after the first main run. What happens here? The ones having made profits from the bottom are now using other people's money. They can afford to try to trade for longer moves of the market. Most people are now expecting the market to go further.

There is credence to the belief that accumulation or distribution is taking place during congestion or choppy areas of the market. (But what about the V bottom or top?) There are markets that defy price pattern prediction for determining when it will end, however. One such market was the long labored move market of live cattle during the early part of 1979, which kept churning upward with only minor corrections. Elliott wave analysts were calling extensions on top of extensions. But there were some clues for those who are knowledgeable. Usually there are fast jerks in the market when accumulation or distribution is taking place. See illustration of

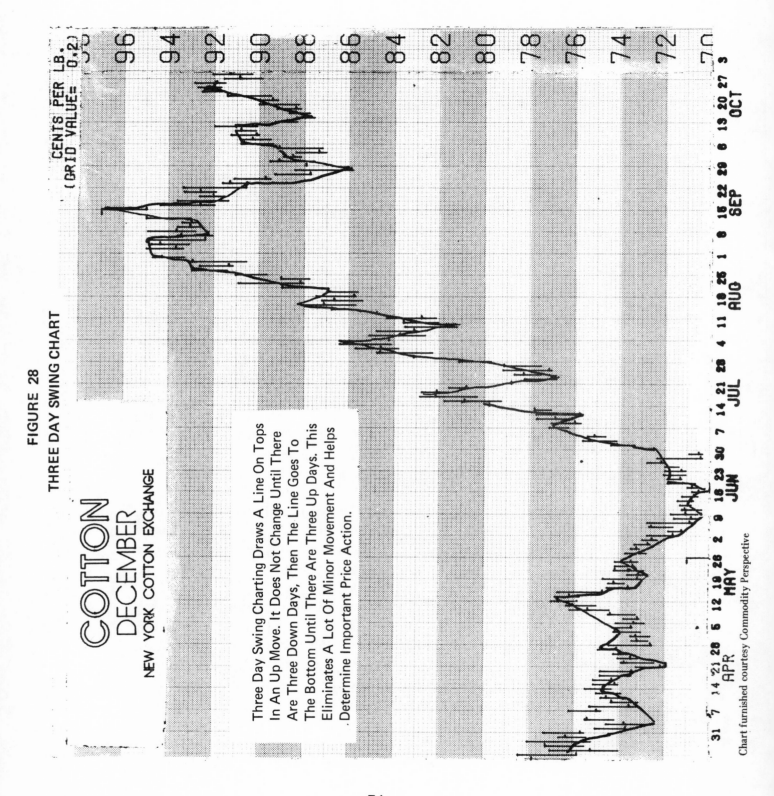

FIGURE 28

THREE DAY SWING CHART

COTTON
DECEMBER
NEW YORK COTTON EXCHANGE

Three Day Swing Charting Draws A Line On Tops In An Up Move. It Does Not Change Until There Are Three Down Days, Then The Line Goes To The Bottom Until There Are Three Up Days. This Eliminates A Lot Of Minor Movement And Helps Determine Important Price Action.

CENTS PER LB.
(GRID VALUE= 0.2)

Chart furnished courtesy Commodity Perspective

74

cotton, Figure 29A. About a month before the end, things began to jerk around a lot more than before. The labored move became more hectic and erratic. It did not swing around a lot, like most topping action, but there were the fast runups and letdowns on occasion (which are another clue to accumulation or distribution).

There are some very large cattle traders. With no limit on how many trades can be put on in a day, as long as the maximum is not exceeded when tallied up after trading hours, big traders can exert a lot of influence in a market on a short term basis. If price shoots up abnormally fast for a day and a half, it can well be big traders driving the market up on a day trade basis, so they can have a higher price to unload their contracts before the end of the day. This is true in many markets (the opposite often works in reverse for accumulation). Part of the reason this can happen is that most of the floor traders know when the big traders are in the pit and are reluctant to trade against them. Since the big traders want to trade fifty-car lots, often they have to do some maneuvering in order to get fills for these orders. The big traders have strength and power on their side, but they leave their tell-tale signs for those who understand. So the fast runup can result when someone is unloading.

HOW HAP FINDS ACCUMULATION AND DISTRIBUTION

1. Look for more than a 30% change over a 10 day moving average in volume for two or more days.

2. Keep a monthly check on the percentage of big traders, in comparison with the change of back months of open interest and in comparison with the ten year averages found in the current Commodity Yearbook.

3. Watch for jerky price patterns, and know that more than likely the price will eventually turn away from the direction of these spike-like chart patterns. See corn illustration, Figure 29B.

4. Keep a total of the times in each short cycle when price moves more than thirty percent over the MA, either up or down. Add the times it goes up, and add the times it goes down; then see if there is a difference between them.

5. Keep the Pressure Index, which will be taught in the next section.

75

FIGURE 29A
SPIKES THAT SHOW ACCUMULATION

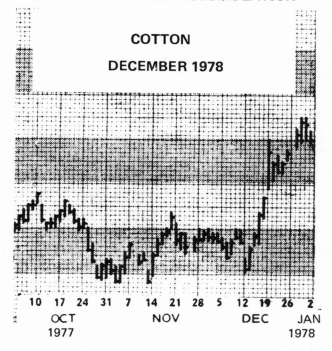

COTTON

DECEMBER 1978

FIGURE 29B
SPIKES THAT SHOW ACCUMULATION

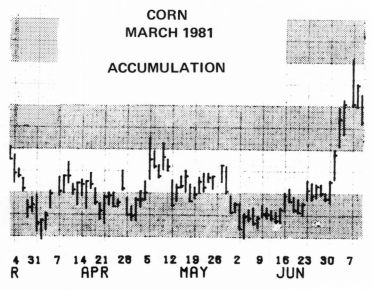

CORN
MARCH 1981

ACCUMULATION

Charts furnished courtesy Commodity Perspective

76

In January 1978, cotton broke out of the churning trading range with spikes that showed accumulation. Was this breakout for real? Or just more churning? To confirm the trade, look at the committment of traders and open interest for that period. Large speculators had increased their positions as of December 31 by ten percent and open interest had increased more than usual. By checking into the seasonal tendencies of cotton, it was confirmed that this was not a time when hedgers generally were going short the market.

It is possible now to go to the Commodity Yearbook and see what is considered normal for hedgers, large speculators and small traders. Traders overlook a good thing if they do not use this information.

THE PRESSURE INDEX OF HAP

Theory: Since we want to eliminate the random movements of the day traders and short-term scalpers, we feel that the market close is the only thing that can judge this. The high and low can be just the pit men running things up and down, but these short-term traders like to get out by the end of the day. So the "close" price should tell what really happened by way of price movement.

The opening price is important because this is where people thought they were in a good trade for the day. These will be proved either right or wrong before the end of the day, for that day's activity. The fact that price is up for the day is not as important as the relationship of the opening with the previous close and the day's close.

For example, if price opens lower than the previous day's close, then goes higher, this means those trading the market earlier were wrong. If it does not go lower for the day but finishes up higher than the previous day, this again means that those trading the market earlier were wrong. Comparing the opening with the former close and the day's close tells you who was right or wrong and filters out the ones who are probably just day traders. In our example, price went down but could not go any further, then came back from the low opening to close higher. We use in our index only the opening price and the close. Price may have run up high or even down low for the day, but we do not use this in our index. We call it HAP's Pressure Index because it tells whether or not the important buying pressure was stronger than the selling pressure. This gives a real clue on what is happening. You can use the theory of Larry Williams' accumulation distribution methods, but use only the open and close.

CALCULATING THE PRESSURE INDEX (FIRST WAY)

1. Make a moving average the length of the short cycle, using close prices.

2. Each day price is up, add the amount of change, from the open to the close, to the moving average amount.

3. If price is down, subtract the amount of change, from the open to the close, from the moving average.

4. Plot these amounts under the same day's price and connect them, creating a line to emphasize the movement.

HOW TO USE THE PRESSURE INDEX

If an oscillator is made of this data, here are the rules to follow: If prices are going up but the index is going down, price will soon go down because there is distribution taking place.

Price should go with the pressure index by the end of the next short cycle period. We have used this many times and it calls the turns regularly. How far this will go before distribution is complete depends on how large the market is and how many contracts have to be quietly unloaded. Total open interest may still be going up, but back open interest should start going down.

When price and the index are moving together, expect price to continue in this direction (see Figure 30).

THE PRESSURE CHART

1. Count the number of days in the short cycle that the close was above the opening; then count the number of days in the short cycle that the close was below the opening (see Figure 30).

2. Add the amounts the opening is above the close and add the amounts the close is below the opening.

Make a chart to more easily keep tabs on the count of the up days and down days. There are four possibilities: 1) Open High and Close Low; 2) Open High and Close High; 3) Open Low and Close Low; 4) Open Low and Close High. We think that when price open contrary to the way it closes, this is extra strong, so double the one that opens high and closes low and the one that opens low and closes high. As the days go by, these four items may be added and summarized. Consider the pressure to be up when the up columns add up to two-thirds more than the down columns. Pressure is down when there are two-thirds more in the down columns (see Figure 30).

FIGURE 30
PRESSURE CHART

DATE	HO-HC	LO-HC	LO-LC	HO-LC
4-2-80				1
4-3-80	1			
4-7-80				1
4-8-80	1			
4-9-82				1
4-10-80	1			
4-15-80		1		
4-16-80				1
4-17-80			1	
4-18-80			1	
4-21-80		1		
4-22-80		1		
4-23-80			1	
4-24-80		1		
	3	4x2	3	4x2
		11		11

FIGURE 31
PRESSURE INDEX CHART

Chart furnished courtesy Commodity Perspective

```
100 CLS:DEFINT I-K,N: DEFSTR A,B:CLEAR 1000
125 REM THIS ROUTINE ENTERS DATA FILE ON WHICH SIM IS TO RUN
150 INPUT"IS THE DATA DISK IN  DRIVE NO. 1";A$
175 INPUT"ENTER FILE NAME ";B$ OPEN"I",1,B$
200 INPUT#1,B$,ND
225 PRINT" READING DATA FILE ";B$;"           ";ND;" DAYS OF DATA"
250 PRINT:PRINT"*****************************************************(***"
275 DIM D(ND+4),W(ND+4),O(ND+4),H(ND+4),L(ND+4),C(ND+4),A(ND+4),N(ND+4),TC(ND+4)
300 FOR I = 1 TO ND
325 INPUT#1,D(I),W(I),O(I),H(I),L(I),C(I)
350 NEXT I
375 PRINT"!!!!!!!!!!!!!!<  ALL DATA ENTERED  >!!!!!!!!!!!!!!!!!!!!!!"
400 INPUT "TURN ON LINE PRINTER AND HIT ENTER";A$
425 CLS:LPRINT"                CONTRACT IS ";B$;"          (";ND;")DAYS DATA"
450 PT=0
475 INPUT"ENTER STARTING DAY NUMBER AND ENDING DAY NUMBER";KS,XX:LPRINT"ENDING DAY NUMBER ";XX;"        DATE ";D(XX)
500 LPRINT" STARTING DAY NUMBER ";KS;"    DATE ";D(KS)
525 PRINT"*********    COMPUTING INDEX  AVG.     *************"
550 LPRINT "DAY";" ";"DATE";" ";"OPEN";" ";"HIGH";" ";"LOW";" ";"CLOSE";" ";"DIFF";TAB(63);"*";"          INDEX"
575 FOR I =KS-14 TO KS
600 D= C(I)-O(I)
625 IF D<0THENR=-D
650 IF D>0THENPO=PO+D
675 MO=MO+R
700 IF MI=0 THEN MI=1
725 PI=PO/14:MI=MO/14:DO=PI/MI
750 LPRINTI;" ";D(I);" ";O(I);" ";H(I);" ";L(I);" ";C(I);" ";D
775 NEXT I
800 PI=PO/14:MI=MO/14:IFMI=0THENMI=1:DO=PI/MI
825 FOR I=KS+1 TO XX
850 D=C(I)-O(I)
875 IF D<0THENR=-D
925 IF D=<0 THEND=0 ELSER=0
950 PI=13*PI/14+D
975 MI=13*MI/14+R
1000 IFMI=0THENMI=1
1025 DO=PI/MI
1050 LL=INT(L(I)*10-600)
1075 HH=INT(H(I)-L(I)+LL)
1200 K=FIX((DO*100+5)/10)
1275 LPRINTD(I);" ";O(I);" ";H(I);" ";L(I);" ";C(I);" ";TAB(LL);TAB(HH);TAB(63);"*";STRINGS(K,35)
1525 NEXT I
1775 INPUT"DO YOU WISH TO CONTINUE <1> OR REVIEW A DAYS DATA <2>";WW
1825 IF WW = 1 GOTO 2775
2275 IFWW=2GOTO 3525
2525 GOTO 1775
2775 KS=XX
3025 XX=XX+25
3275 GOTO 825
3525 INPUT "ENTER STARTING DAY NUMBER AND ENDING DAY NUMBER TO BE REVIEWED";SS,EE
3775 INPUT"DO YOU WISH A PRINTOUT<Y>OR<N>  ";P$
4025 IF P$="Y" THEN GOTO 5275
4275 PRINT"NO. ";"DATE","OPEN","HIGH","LOW","CLOSE"
4525 FOR I=SSTOEE
4775 PRINTI;" ";D(I),O(I),H(I),L(I),C(I)
4925 NEXTI
5275 FORI=SSTOEE
5525 LPRINT"DAY NO. ","DATE","OPEN","HIGH","LOW","CLOSE","DIFF"
5775 LPRINTI,D(I),O(I),H(I),L(I),C(I),C(I)-O(I)
6025 NEXT I
6275 GOTO 1775
```

81

CHAPTER 5

THE MEDIAN LINE METHOD

Dr. Allan Andrews sent us letters twice saying that we could use this F.F.E.S. technique in our writings. Since we ordinarily use only our own work, we have not included it before. Now we note that some writers are using his median line technique without giving him credit. We think Dr. Andrews is one of the best market analysts and has made a real contribution to the field of market analysis; so we want to give credit to Dr. Andrews and let people know that this technique was invented and propagated by him.

Dr. A.H. Andrews, of the Foundation for Economic Stabilization, conceived this method as a better way to use W.D. Gann's angle system on any kind of chart, rather than only charts scaled on a one-to-one basis. He called it the "Median Line Method." The basic idea is to draw a line from a pivot through the middle of the next swing. Those who have studied the Gann method of bringing angle lines up or down from turning points have probably noticed how many times one of the lines will go through the middle of a swing on out to the top or bottom of another pivot.

The following examples show four of the ML's. Note that ML-4-5, A went on beyond the line an equal distance as it took to get to the line. See that Ax is equal to xB on the graph on Figure 32.

The median line goes from a turning point through the middle of the next swing, as shown in Figure 32 where the line starts at "O" and goes through the swing pivots one and two. There must be three swings to start.

FIGURE 32
MEDIAN LINES

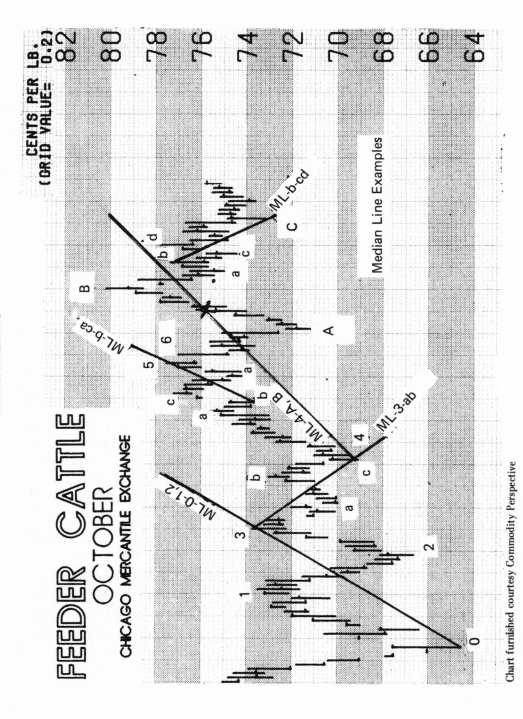

Chart furnished courtesy Commodity Perspective

84

THEORY USED ON MEDIAN LINES

1. Elliott Wave count is necessary and part of the method. Use this method on zig-zag price patterns. Flat patterns or irregular patterns do not work with enough regularity.

2. Elliott count of the #5 leg is expected to be the end; and traders are instructed to bring up stops or exit the trade here.

3. Other action-reaction methods are used along with this method, such as the 0-3 and 0-4 techniques, the expanding pivot technique, converging lines method, or spiral count.

4. Followers of this method are instructed to get work done on weeklies for main trends in order to know the best trades. There are about ten techniques involved with the action-reaction method. This median line technique is only one. Use a number of these methods or techniques before taking a trade.

In using the median line, one must make a line from the third pivot back. At times this means that a small swing is used with a large one. Always use the last three swings and their turning point. If there has been a gap, this is counted as a pivot, since price jumped over what would normally have been a pivot. If price goes toward a ML a lot faster than normal, the ML is not expected to hold. The trader must count the number of days it ordinarily takes for a certain commodity to go a specific distance; then when this is exceeded by fifty percent or more, it is known that there is extra momentum and strength behind the move and the lines should not be expected to hold. When the ML is penetrated, a line an equal distance out is drawn . This third line is called the "Warning Line." As long as price continues at a velocity of fifty percent, or more, faster than normal, reaction trades are not made. There are ten rules that must be followed when using this method. Do not trade against a sharp or steep angle going up (or down) in a runaway market.

RULES FOR TRADING THE MEDIAN LINES

1. Use the weeklies first.
2. Use at least three or more action-reaction techniques to verify a trade.

3. Failures to reach a line may be traded in the opposite direction, as this is a sign of weakness.

4. For every action, there should be an equal reaction. Pivots spaced apart in an up move should have about the same spacing in the following down move.

5. Price converging with two multi-pivot lines should see a reversal, at least temporarily.

6. Use Elliott Wave count to help entry and exit.

7. On flat or irregular markets, use mini-Median lines through closes and only trade short term, or not at all.

8. Spiral count on ten degree angles, coming down from tops and up from bottoms, will help. Pay attention when these lines cross.

9. Velocity must be kept in mind in case of a runaway market not holding at lines where it normally should.

10. Certain markets work better than others. Bellies do not work as well with this method; nor does any especially thin market. Use the nearest month when possible, or the one with the largest open-interest. Price must be swinging enough to give these techniques a chance to work.

F.F.E.S.—REVERSE MEDIAN LINES

These are lines coming from the middle of a swing under a pivot, extending on out to price action. The line could also come from the middle of a swing over the top of the next pivot to extend out where it may be in line with future price action (see Figure 33). They usually find the next pivot and make reliable center lines for the action-reaction method.

Reverse median lines have the same rules as the median lines and are used the same way. Both ML and RML are useful. Work on an acetate overlay so there will not be too many lines on the chart. With practice, skill is developed in recognizing the patterns and how to best use the lines on each different one; but until this is accomplished, the transparent overlay will let several different trials be attempted until the right one is found.

FIGURE 33
REVERSE MEDIAN LINES

PORK BELLIES
JULY
CHICAGO MERCANTILE EXCHANGE

CONTRACT PBN 80
HIGH   58.85:11/21/79
LOW   31.95:04/18/80
        AS OF THURS.

CENTS PER LB.
(GRID VALUE= 0.2)

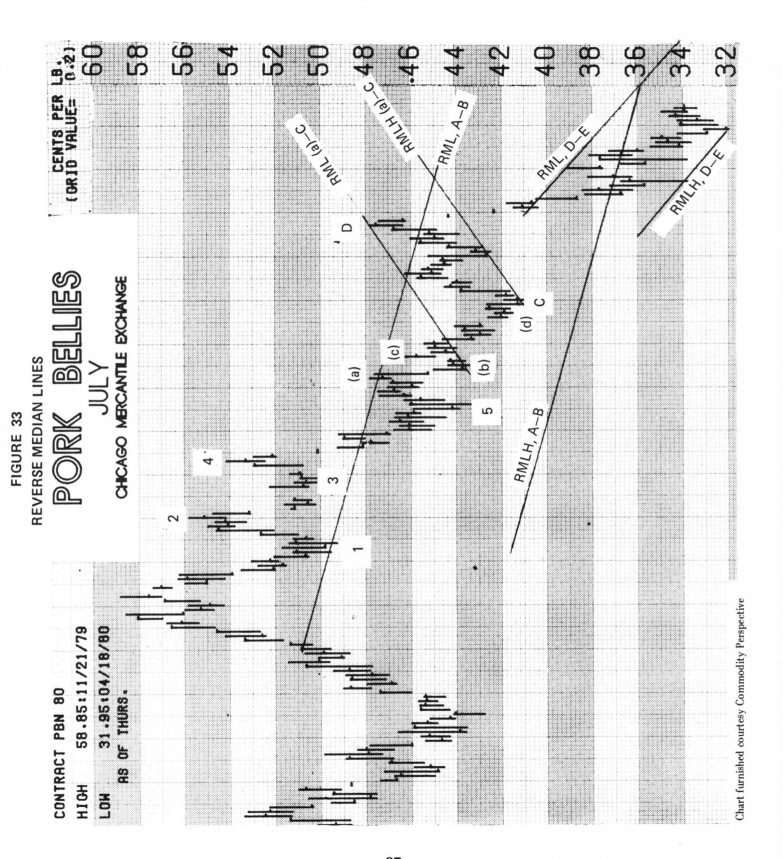

Chart furnished courtesy Commodity Perspective

87

FIGURE 34
REVERSE MEDIAN LINES

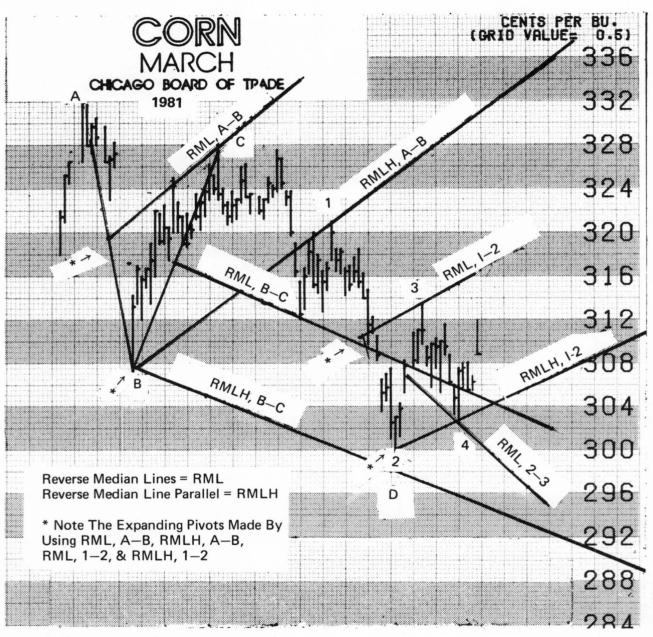

Chart furnished courtesy Commodity Perspective

88

FIGURE 35

MEDIAN LINES WITH EXPANDING PIVOT LINES

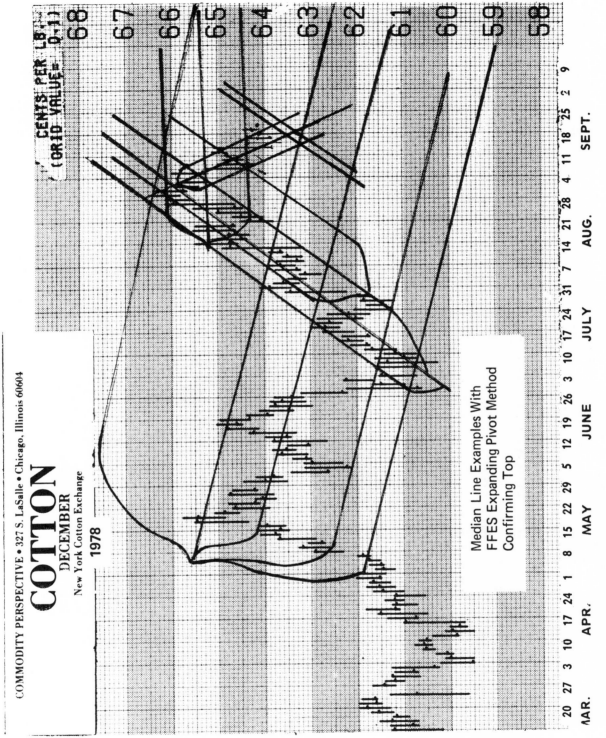

COMMODITY PERSPECTIVE • 327 S. LaSalle • Chicago, Illinois 60604

COTTON
DECEMBER
New York Cotton Exchange
1978

CENTS PER LB.
(GRID VALUE= 0.1)

Median Line Examples With
FFES Expanding Pivot Method
Confirming Top

Chart furnished courtesy Commodity Perspective

89

FIGURE 36
MINI-MEDIAN LINES

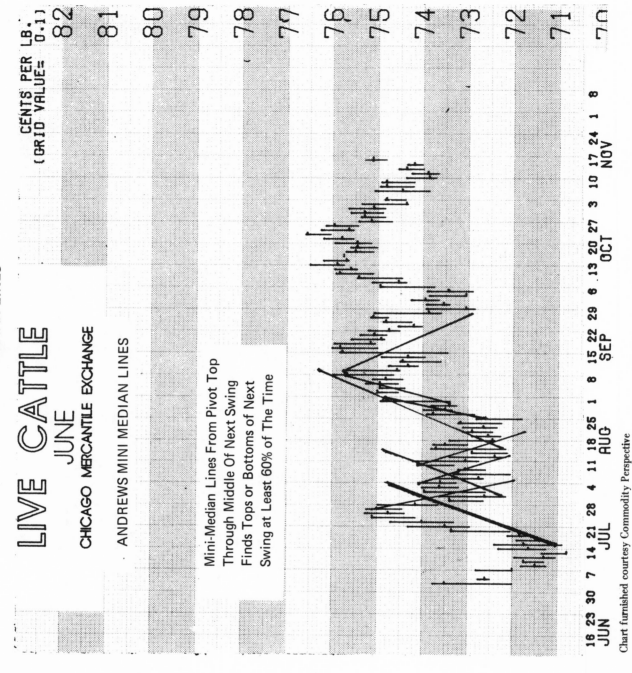

LIVE CATTLE
JUNE
CHICAGO MERCANTILE EXCHANGE

ANDREWS MINI MEDIAN LINES

CENTS PER LB.
(GRID VALUE= 0.1)

Mini-Median Lines From Pivot Top
Through Middle Of Next Swing
Finds Tops or Bottoms of Next
Swing at Least 60% of The Time

CHAPTER 6

THE RHYTHM METHOD OF TRADING

THEORY USED

The theory behind this plan is to learn to count the ebb and flow of the market, then get into swing with it. This is more easily understood when the kind of market is known. It works best in large congestion areas, choppy markets, or channels. Speed should be considered, along with characteristics (such as jerks or spikes). Study previous areas similar to the one being traded to know what may happen again.

The repetition of turning points on a certain number of trading days is expected. This is not the same as a cycle, which goes by time periods. There are periods when the market will trade in repetitious patterns, with a certain number of days between pivots. The distance up or down is not the determining factor in these instances.

There is often a break in the larger rhythm that is about half of the main rhythm amount. The rhythm count should alternate some between one-half of the count, and twice the count. For example, the meats are usually on a rhythm of ten days and five days, but there may be a number of three or two-day minor turns within these larger ones. On faster momentum expect the larger count of ten, and in slower markets expect more of the fives and threes or twos (see Figure 37).

FIGURE 37
RHYTHM COUNT

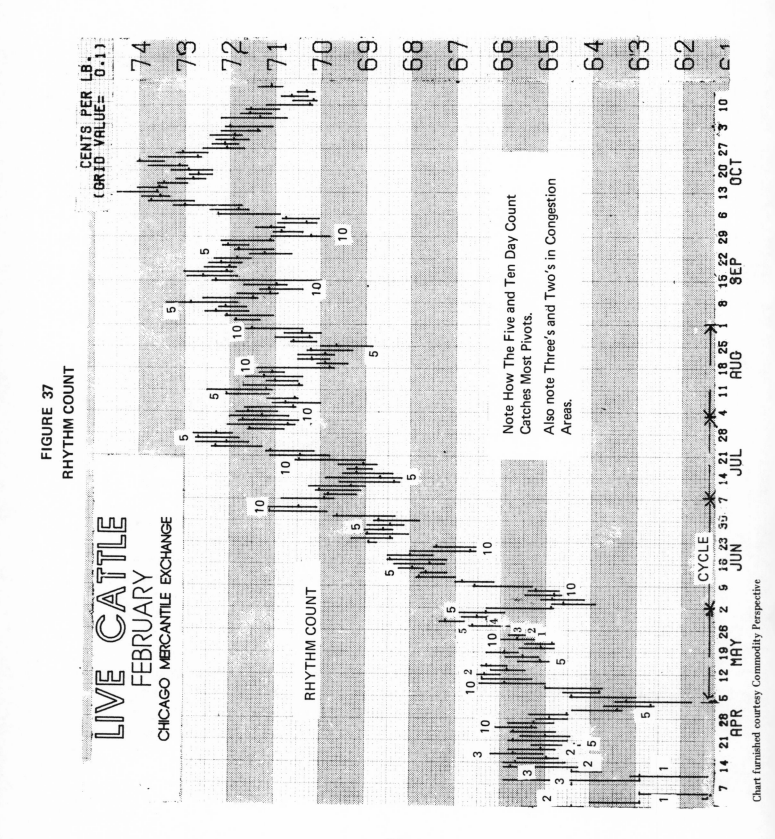

LIVE CATTLE
FEBRUARY
CHICAGO MERCANTILE EXCHANGE

CENTS PER LB.
(GRID VALUE= 0.1)

RHYTHM COUNT

Note How The Five and Ten Day Count Catches Most Pivots.

Also note Three's and Two's in Congestion Areas.

Chart furnished courtesy Commodity Perspective

92

HOW TO FIND THE RHYTHM COUNT

1. Use the fifty percent rule on as many old highs and lows (or congestion areas) as possible to find a cluster of these close together. The fifty percent rule can be calculated on time as well as price; so find and use the price at the halfway point in time. Average these cluster numbers to get one spot to use in beginning the count. It will be amazing how many times this cluster average spot comes at some important turning point on the price chart.

Look at the illustration of February Cattle on Figure 37. It took six weeks, from 2/23 to 4/3/80, for price to come down from 73.50 to 61.50 (twelve cents down). Halfway back up would be at 67.50. Half of six weeks, or three weeks (April 24), was when February Cattle reversed to come back to its base. Halfway from the low on June 3 at 64.00 and the high on July 3 is 67.50. (It went seven cents, so add three and one-half to sixty four). This makes 67.50 twice. The one-half time period brought over to April 24 makes a cluster of three here at this point. Note on the chart where the count of ten came out correct to verify this as the place to start the count again.

To balance time, six weeks over and six spaces up from the double bottom is May 21. See the pivot on May 21. This same process can be repeated using the small swings, spotting equal amounts down and over, and half amounts down and over. For a runaway, as described above where the market came down twelve cents rapidly, the small congestion areas may be used. These may be found quickly by marking a transparent ruler with a felt pen.

2. Since it is expected that the rhythm will come out on some turning points, cycles can be used to help find the starting place. When several cycles come out at one place, this should be where to start counting. This is illustrated by the marks at the bottom of Figure 38.

3. A turning point that appears to be major is usually a place to start. These should be main highs or lows.

4. Count from some high back to a low, then count from the low to the high, noting the number of days that are close to the same count from each direction. The rhythm will soon be found. It may go off some for one (or maybe even two) days, but should stay the same most of the time.

93

5. Note the count going with a channel, and the count against the channel (or action-reaction count).

6. Elliott Wave count may be used to help tell where to start and when to expect turns. The Elliott "Flat" and "Irregular or Triangle" type of market is best for this method. The Elliott rule of alternates should help the trader expect these patterns. Note the Roman numerals on the chart on Figure 38.

7. Use of the HAP congestion finding methods will help start the rhythm count as a leg or swing turns into a congestion area.

WHERE THIS ORIGINATED

Earlier methods of rhythm were used by Pugh, but the markets were slower fifty years ago during the depression. Eugene Nofri used the technique with some variations. His method is called the Nofri Congestion Phase System. W.D. Gann knew about this and exhorted his followers to learn the average number of days in swings, movements, and reactions of the market. A few old traders understood these principles and passed them along in their families. In 1976, it was explained to the author by a trader in Houston. At that time the rhythm for beans was three days, three weeks, or three months with the large rhythm count correcting any lack of evenness in the smaller count. This trader showed his results and he made a lot of money with this method. Occasionally, some trader will discover this idea in his research of the market and get excited about it. Several versions of it have been circulated around over the years. R.N. Elliott had a lot to say about the rhythm of the market, but he worked mostly with indexes, like the Dow Jones.

HOW TO TRADE WITH THE RHYTHM METHOD

1. To get started, find the rhythm and know the kind of market in progress. Is it a congestion, or just choppy swings with small congestion areas? The way things start will generally continue long enough to make money. Have the stage, level and kind of market clearly in mind. They each must be traded a little different.

FIGURE 38
RHYTHM COUNT AND CHANNELS

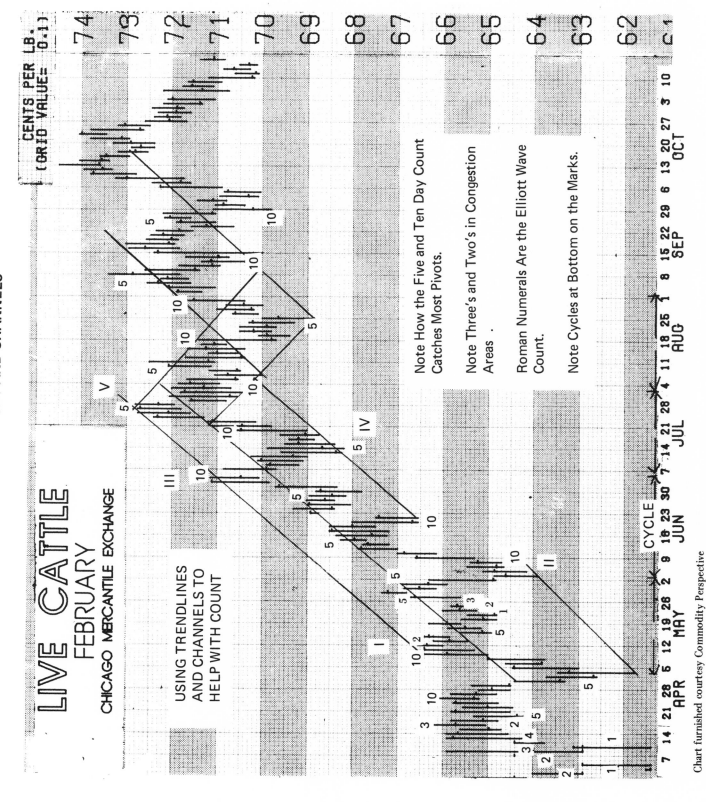

LIVE CATTLE
FEBRUARY
CHICAGO MERCANTILE EXCHANGE

CENTS PER LB.
(GRID VALUE= 0.1)

USING TRENDLINES
AND CHANNELS TO
HELP WITH COUNT

Note How the Five and Ten Day Count
Catches Most Pivots.

Note Three's and Two's in Congestion
Areas .

Roman Numerals Are the Elliott Wave
Count.

Note Cycles at Bottom on the Marks.

Chart furnished courtesy Commodity Perspective

95

2. Rhythm in the Congestion Phase

Here there are only highs and lows with which to work. There are no old highs or lows, and trendlines are only across tops and bottoms. But usually there are small spikes up and down within the congestion area. These spikes are the two or three day upturns, with a reverse and downturn for the bottom spike. After counting many of these spikes, it is found that there are usually only three before a breakout. Sometimes the breakout comes back into the congestion area, however, and some larger spikes evolve in a bigger congestion channel (see Figure 7, May Oats chart in "Pivot Finder Lines" section).

Short term rhythm is used here. It is best to only trade for one-half of the short rhythm unless the area is broad. Expect stops to be run occasionally, which will cause the channel to be violated. Conservative traders wait for the second day of a breakout for validation, unless there is other good evidence to back up the move. If the rhythm is five days, it is best to only try to take three days out of this while in the congestion area. Do not trade if the congestion is narrow, where there is not enough room (to go in and out safely with profits) to warrant the risk. Some rhythm methods advocate doubling up if the market goes bad. We think the small trader should get out if price comes back through his entry point. Take a small loss and try again later.

3. Rhythm in the Choppy Market

This market allows the use of short trend lines and previous highs or lows. If this market is going up and down in a well-defined manner, channel lines may be better. With these alterations for this type of zig-zag market, the trader may stay in longer, using the trendline or channel line to get out or reverse. Do not reverse until the long count has been reached in a more swinging type of market. The count of ten for meats will probably see some turns on threes and fives. Keep the main rhythm clearly in mind as guiding spots for reversals and times to trade in the other direction. If this is merely a flat in a larger zig-zag pattern, it is safer to trade with the main trend; or take smaller bites of the market when going in the opposite direction.

In trading with the trend, stay with the trade as long as the old highs are being taken out. Traders may decide whether or not they want to let the market go against them in hopes that the upward swings will continue, rather than get out with a close trend line. Regardless of profits or desire to make a longer term trade, when old lows or highs are taken out and price reverses, the trader should exit or roll over the trade.

This kind of trading is expecially good for using Elliott Wave count, Fibonacci numbers and Pivot Finder techniques to anticipate a breakout. When several of these indicators agree, it is best to keep in this market as long as possible, in hopes of being in on a big move out of the choppy market.

Rhythm does not indicate the direction for the market and has no way of indicating the amplitude of the move. Sometimes the change in rhythm is a break from a congestion or choppy area. So keep track of other indicators to help you stay in for the bigger moves. Sliding parallel stops work well with this. See the horizontal lines in the illustration below.

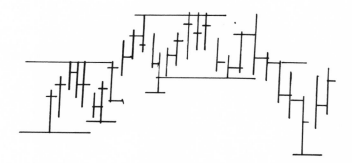

Buy or sell areas may reverse on occasion. There may be some whipsawing, but this should be kept to a minimum if a break-even type of trade is used, getting out when the market pulls back to the entry point. This should be on an "on-close only" basis unless the market is showing unusual velocity.

Failure to reach a congestion line or channel line is an indication of strength in a market and means that price should go further than it did on the previous move.

97

4. The Swinging Market

These are usually found in higher price areas with a larger than usual open interest. Markets swing a lot more these days, with so many more trading and political rumors abounding. If this market is near a low or in an area suspected to be a top, accumulation/distribution techniques must be used.

If not near a top area or a bottom area, the long count may be taken in these markets, as long as sliding stops are used. If near a top or bottom area, (or where one is suspected) only trade the short rhythm count. Even better, trade with the expected main move.

If a runaway market develops, expect the long count to be reached and only look for two-day reactions.

VALUE OF USING RHYTHM

This method, combined with time and price techniques, such as balancing and cycles, makes one of the best market tools. Other indicators should be used, but this technique will give a trader a definite edge.

CHAPTER 7

THE CLOSELINE METHOD

People used clothes lines and clothes pins back in the old days. Clothes pins were ordinarily left on the line. Clothes of the same size were put together and the pins were left to be handy. These patterns of pins spaced at various distances made the work easier. Instead of clothes lines, we are interested in "close" lines, or cases when the close of a commodity will fall into a line. If traders will learn to use the close of a market properly, this will make his work easier and better.

WHY CLOSES ARE MORE IMPORTANT

Day traders try to exit the market before the close. Often the run from high to low of the daily thrust is greatly exaggerated by day traders. Since they ordinarily get out before the close, the close is more important than the high or low and represents the true change from the previous day. Using the close, the dominant part of the commodity chart filters out the extraneous trades; and, when interpreted properly, will tell the trader what really counts in a market.

Some of the most successful traders only use the close in their work. We could give examples such as Graham Loving, Jr., but the important thing is to let a trader see for himself.

The Closeline Method

WHAT IS EXPECTED IN CLOSELINE TRADING

Refer to Figure 39 for the following points.

1. Note the distances between closes. Are they even distances apart and fairly regular in spacing?

2. Pay special attention to closes that are unusually far apart or more close together than usual.

3. Take a ruler and make a light line connecting closes that go straight. Note how the lines often indicate a small trend in the market.

4. Note when a close is off the line. Is it above or below (to the left or to the right of the line)?

5. Draw a circle around clusters close together, especially if going lateral or sideways. These will be congestion areas.

6. Have a way to remember the sharpness or flatness of angle by making a transparent overlay of the repetitious angle.

WHAT OTHERS HAVE DONE

1. Trendline traders have used close-only lines for a long time.

2. Momentum theory uses the degree of angle to predict the amount of momentum or velocity of the market.

3. The amount of thrust has been gauged in various ways by analysts to show reversal patterns, or weakness and strength of a market.

4. The closeline method does not need special charts. The difference is in the angle of travel from a turning point during a swing. The closeline is simple, but has proven good with the rules below put into practice.

THEORY BEHIND THE CLOSELINE METHOD

1. Momentum.
2. Trendline use.
3. Fifty percent rule.
4. Angles less than thirty degrees are considered weak; and angles more than sixty degrees are considered strong, but sharp angles near a turn are not to be trusted as the correct angle.
5. Time and price balancing.

100

FIGURE 39

CLOSE LINE CHARTING

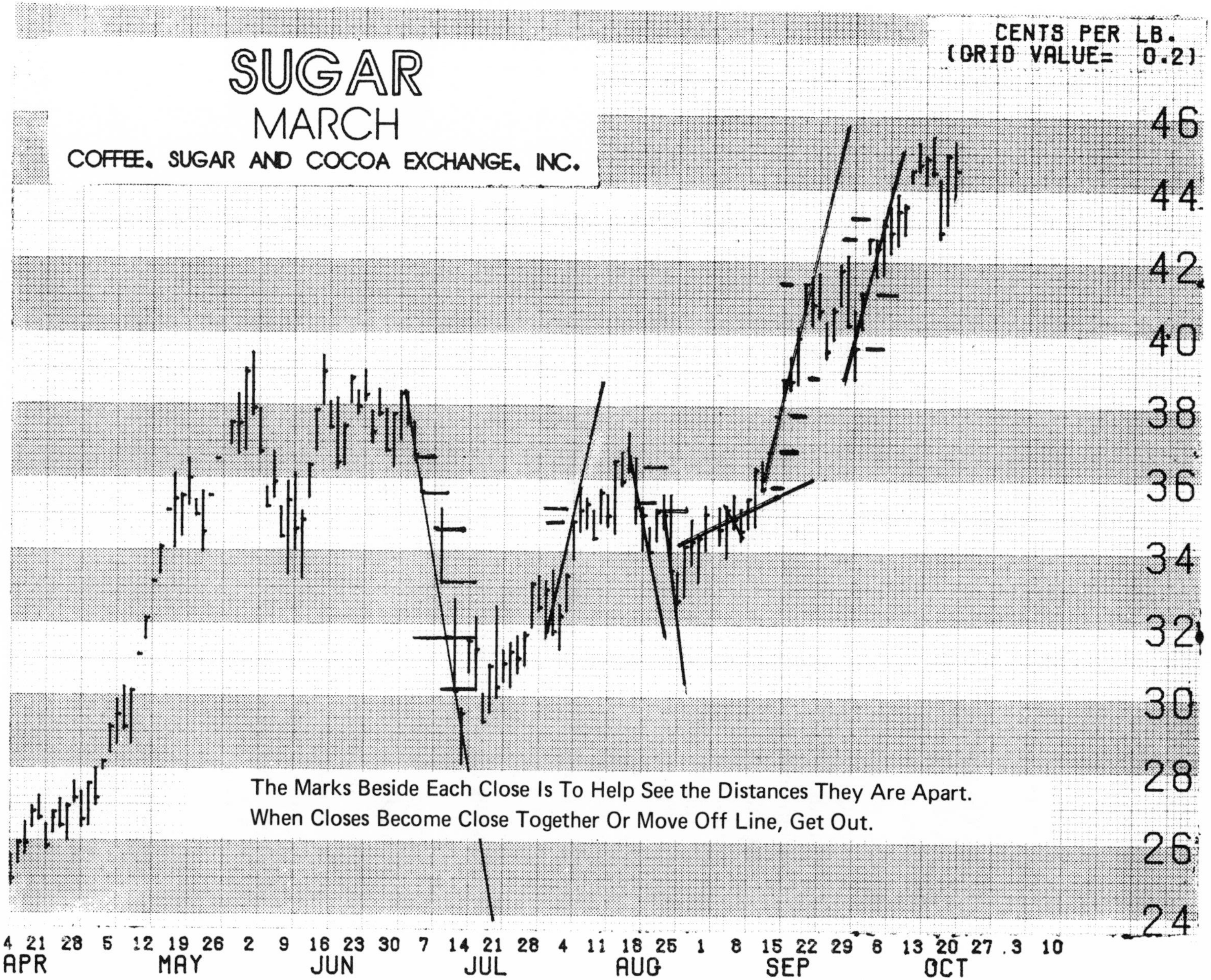

SUGAR
MARCH
COFFEE, SUGAR AND COCOA EXCHANGE, INC.

CENTS PER LB.
(GRID VALUE= 0.2)

46
44
42
40
38
36
34
32
30
28
26
24

4 21 28 5 12 19 26 2 9 16 23 30 7 14 21 28 4 11 18 25 1 8 15 22 29 8 13 20 27 3 10
APR   MAY   JUN   JUL   AUG   SEP   OCT

The Marks Beside Each Close Is To Help See the Distances They Are Apart.
When Closes Become Close Together Or Move Off Line, Get Out.

Chart furnished courtesy Commodity Perspective

101

6. Ordinary charts may be used with close accentuated for updating.

HOW TO USE IN TRADING

1. Go back over previous charts to learn the normal rate of movement between closes while in a swing. These often will be close to an average distance apart and will show a normal market, consisting of four or five days or closes remaining about the same distance apart. Each market will have its own common spacing for closes. These must be catalogued and learned so they can be used as needed. Various commodities will show certain spacing between closes when in similar kinds of markets or price patterns. This is another repetitious pattern of the market to be used for profits. Different seasons will show different spacing in some commodities at regular times each year.

2. This is swing trading. Note the angle of change coming from the previous line of travel or break from a congestion. Sharp angles over sixty degrees are not to be used unless the market is already in a runaway movement. If other reversal indicators agree, these sharp angles may be traded, but expect a pullback soon and a closeline being on a more normal angle. After the pullback has been reversed, find the line of travel by skipping the closes of this sharp initial move to make the closeline.

A flat angle is to be suspected, unless the market has previously been moving on similar flat angles and is near historical lows where price is normally not volatile or active. Flat angles with closes spaced near each other will probably be congestions or short choppy swings. Use an angle of about forty-five degrees. In bear markets, the normal angle should be about ten degrees more, or a fifty-five degree angle line down. Use average angle techniques for more accurate interpretation (see Chapter 13).

3. When the market moves on the proper angle with normal distances, make the line on two closing prices and trade with this line as the guide. As long as the close stays above or to the left of the line in an up market, this is all right, unless there is too large a change in the normal distances between the closing prices (see the lines on Figure 30). Expect five, and usually only four, closing prices to stay on (or above) the line. If the price goes the distance expected more rapidly, profits should be taken. Time and price balancing rules, taught elsewhere in this book, should be used. If the angle

is flat, a more sharp movement to balance price may occur, but swings should not be large until a pattern emerges that is not so flat.

4. Recurring angle methods help, but use the distances between closes as a momentum indicator.

5. This is primarily a short-term method, but the long-term trader can use these principles with weekly charts.

6. To summarize, find two closes that are about the normal distance apart. Expect price to go twice this distance. If a close moves to the right of the line, get out of a trade. If the close jumps, covering the expected space about twice as fast, take profits. There should normally be four closes on the line or to the left before a change.

7. Other indicators should be used to reinforce this method. It uses average angle, time and price balancing, momentum and trendline theory just as they are used elsewhere. This is an important part of the complete trading information needed to consistently make money in the market. Find as many indicators as possible to back up a trade.

PROGRAM FOR TRADING THE "CLOSELINE"

1. a. If a close is above (or below) clusters or nests of other closes;

   b. If there are two evenly spaced closes away from the last close in the cluster, draw a line through them;

   c. If the angle of travel is:

      1. going up above a 45° angle or

      2. going down below a 45° angle, this is a strong trade indication.

2. Exceptions:

   a. If a congestion area exists and the angle is:

      1) going up more than 65°

      2) going down more than 70°

   b. If it moves too fast look for a pull back. If there is a pull back followed by a continuation, make a new line;

   c. If there is a crest shortly above (or below) the break from the cluster;

3. Exit if the close is to be to the right of the line (the first two evenly spaced X's).

4. The target is twice the distance of travel of the first two line days. If it goes this fast the first day, either exit or bring the top in close for profits.

5. Closes must be going on a straight line and evenly spaced apart to show sustained support and momentum.

a. If the space is to be twice as close as usual, exit or bring in stops close for profits.

b. If the space between closes is twice as far apart, expect this to be an exhaust, and exit or bring in stops close for profits.

6. If there are three evenly spaced closes in a straight line, out of the cluster more than 30° but less than 45°, this may be traded using the same rules as above. The reverse is true for going down. It must be more than 30° and less than 45°. This may occur when the market has been rather flat previously.

CHAPTER 8

DAY TRADING METHODS

WHAT HAS BEEN TRIED IN THE PAST

1. An old formula that has been used with a lot of variations is to average the high, low, and close for the day; then use this with constants, Fibonacci ratios, or other factors believed to be relevant to try to estimate the next day's price range.

2. Another idea that has been around a long time is to take the differences between two moving averages on several time intervals and use this to project a future price.

3. The CRAM method gets the best fit of a curve's travel, and projects this out to predict a new price.

4. Several methods use the previous high, low, and close numbers as support or resistance areas for the next day's price action. Old highs and lows are utilized, helping this work better than most other methods.

5. There have been a lot of other methods that have been used, such as the Taylor system, that have apparently proven helpful to their users.

WHAT REALLY WORKS

What turned the bad record of day trading around was the discovery by John R. Hill of Hendersonville, N.C. that five minute charts made up as the day progresses could be used the same as on daily charts. Now the reliable daily indicators could be used on an intraday basis with just as much success. What works on the daily charts will also work on the five minute charts. If things do not work on the five minute charts, they will not work on the longer term ones either. A lot of appreciation is due John Hill for his efforts to educate traders. Now all one has to do is adjust the timing tools and money control methods to the intraday trading scale.

THE TIMING OF DAY TRADING

1. Key Times to Watch
    a. Opening—for evaluation.
    b. Twenty-five to forty minutes after opening, there should be a correction.
    c. Mid-morning or on coffee break for pit traders.
    d. An hour before the close, which should see the trend of the day resume.

2. If trading against the trend, wait about twenty-five minutes after the opening to enter.

3. H-B time — if the market makes new highs (or new lows) in the last forty minutes of trading, it should be expected to continue further the next day and should be a good overnight trade.

4. Ask the broker to find out the usual coffee break time for each pit you are trading and do not initiate a trade during this time.

5. Expect a reversal about sixty-five percent of the time around an hour and forty-five minutes after the opening, if the market has been moving fairly steady in one direction until then.

6. Expect the market to change back to the main trend about two and one-half to three hours after the opening.

EXAMPLE OF DAY TRADING METHOD

1. If price goes above yesterday's high when not in a congestion area then comes back below it, sell; if price goes below yesterday's low, then comes back above it, buy.

2. If price opens up from the previous close, wait for the pull back to

buy; if price opens down from the previous close, wait for the pull back to sell. (Do this unless rule 1, previously listed, is violated).

3. If long, and price fails to go above the previous day's high, get out; or if short, and price fails to go below the previous day's low, get out. Wait for rule 1 or 2, above, to put you back in the market.

4. If price comes down below both the high and close, reverse positons immediately; if price goes up above both the low and close when short, reverse immediately.

5. Favor direction of the main trend.

6. If there is an average swing day moving about the same as other swing days in the trend direction, stay in the market.

7. Do not get out until the previous day's high (or low) is violated; or has a failure on the opening.

8. If price goes more than thirty-eight point above or below a high or low, expect a continuation.

9. If closing will be more than halfway from the day's high (or low), get out; or reverse, if the trend favors that direction.

10. Take old highs and lows back for five or ten days, looking for resistance and support lines. Use these with the same rules as above on previous day's high, low and close.

Refer to, *Scientific Interpretation of Bar Charts,* by John R. Hill for more help on this method.

EXAMPLE OF DAY TRADING

Note: This method was developed with the help of J.L. Patterson.

Using Pivot Finder Lines

Rule 1. Do not trade the first ten minutes after a commodity opens. Wait until the market settles down.

Rule 2. Trade only if the market is moving in an orderly manner. Do not trade in a grasshopper, gyrating or hectic market.

Rule 3. Trade in a trigger area in the direction of the target area. If a commodity goes through a target area without showing any resistance whatsoever, place limit order to go into the market. This must be sent directly to the floor and not by wire to avoid too much time loss. Limit the order by ten points and as soon as there is a fill with confirmation, put in the opposite order, earning twenty percent on invested capital. For example: on a day trade, if you have to put up eight hundred dollars to play cattle, then it takes forty points in order to receive twenty percent on the invested capital. If you get filled at a better percent, this is fine. Let's say you are trading at 53.10 and you limit your order between 53.10 and 53.20. You can then place a sell order, assuming you had just bought 40 points above 53.10, or 53.50. If you get filled below 53.10, that's extra profits.

Rule 4. Do not trade against the balance point trend indicator.

Rule 5. Draw Pivot Finder lines ahead of price action on five minute charts. Mini ML's may also be used.

Rule 6. Do not trade against leaders. Example A: Do not short Live Cattle if Feeder Cattle are going straight up. Example B: Do not short Meal if the Beans are going strong in the opposite direction.

Rule 7. Do not try to take more than 20% profit on investment per day trade. Many times greater profits can be taken, but your risk grows exponentially as you leave the 20% area.

Rule 8. You should not be in overnight, since a good close would hit your target and a poor close is negative, except when the market makes a move in your favor in the last thirty minutes of trading time.

Rule 9. If you decide to get out of a position, do it at a controlled price, never at market orders.

Rule 10. Never invest more than 10% of trading capital in any one position on a day trade.

Rule 11. If you have three trades working, wait until one of the previous trades is out before putting on a new trade during trading hours.

Rule 12. Do not use stops, but get out if stop amount listed below is hit.

Rule 13. Trade only with the trend after 12 A.M.

Rule 14. Do not trade after up limit day or down limit day.

Rule 15. If price goes back through previous swing low (or previous swing high), get out early.

Rule 16. If there is an extra fast move, get out. (Sudden jerks mean accumulation; or, at times, other shorts or longs running for cover). If we are in an area for stops, this is an exception. When stops are run, it should come back.

Rule 17. If there is a PF line, buy; but if it is not above previous lows, stay out.

Rule 18. If it signals a target to sell that is not below previous high, stay out.

FIGURE 40

REVERSAL DAY SIGNALS

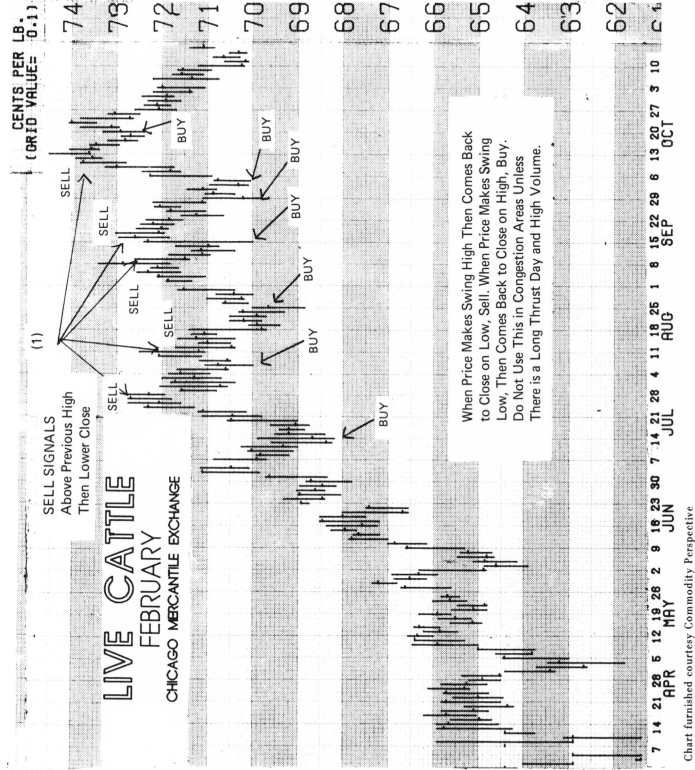

SELL SIGNALS
Above Previous High
Then Lower Close

When Price Makes Swing High Then Comes Back
to Close on Low, Sell. When Price Makes Swing
Low, Then Comes Back to Close on High, Buy.
Do Not Use This in Congestion Areas Unless
There is a Long Thrust Day and High Volume.

CENTS PER LB.
(GRID VALUE= 0.1)

LIVE CATTLE
FEBRUARY
CHICAGO MERCANTILE EXCHANGE

Chart furnished courtesy Commodity Perspective

109

FIGURE 41

DAY TRADING SUGGESTED AMOUNTS

SUGGESTED AMOUNTS
(Margins May Change, However)

	Commodity	Margin	Fudge Factor	Stop	Amount Per Tic	20% of Margin	Target
1)	Live Cattle	1,000	.15	.25 pts	4.00	200.00	.50
2)	Feeder Cattle	1,200	.15	.25 pts	4.20	240.00	.60
3)	Live Hogs	900	.15	.20 pts	3.00	180.00	.60
4)	Pork Bellies	1,500	.25	.40 pts	3.80	300.00	.75
5)	Beans	1,500	.03	3½¢	12.50	300.00	.05
6)	Wheat	1,200	.02	2½¢	12.50	240.00	.05
7)	T-Bills	2,000	.05	.6 pts	25.00	400.00	.17
8)	Deutschemark	1,500	.10	.15 pts	12.50	300.00	.0035
9)	Swiss Frank	2,000	.15	.20 pts	12.50	600.00	.0070
10)	Copper	1,200	.30	.35 pts	2.50	240.00	.75

CHAPTER 9

GOING IN OR OUT

BEST MONTH TO TRADE

1. In an inverted market with the front months the strongest, buy a front month and plan to roll forward.

2. In a carrying charge market, where the back months are progressively higher in price; for selling, pick the month with the largest open interest. The back months with large open interest are more apt to be where the commercials are shorting.

3. Find what the hedgers are doing by comparing open interest changes between near and back months, as described earlier. Subscribe to a hedgers' advisory report or service that is widely followed. Learn why the producers hedge, when they hedge and how they hedge.

4. Buy a premium market breakout, but be leery of a discount market breakout.

5. The month that is the slowest to go up is often the fastest to go down, when the market turns around.

6. Compare markets with the same month of a commodity, such as wheat and corn.

BUYING ON NEWS OR REPORTS

1. Estimates of a report's impact on the market are often proven wrong.

2. If the market fails to act on news the way it should, this is a good signal to do the opposite.

3. If there have been two weak USDA reports with the market falling fast, the third report should see a reaction. This usually occurs when advance estimates are bright expectations in the direction of the bias of the former reports.

USING PRICE PATTERNS TO ENTER

1. A three-point equilibrium reversal should be entered at the close on the third day, especially if accompanied by high volume.

2. One-day reversals must have other indicators to be dependable. They should have high volume, plus a long thrust in the direction indicated, and also open in the indicated direction the following day.

3. The pullback of a rally that exceeds the normal time (not price) of other pullbacks or corrections is a warning that a reversal may be coming.

4. An ABC correction is a good entrance pattern. With price not going beyond old highs (or lows), go in on the "C" turn. This is sometimes called the coiled spring pattern. It is especially good when the back months verify (see Figure 42).

5. After a long move in one direction, a reversal followed by a gap is usually a good trade (see Figure 43).

6. Price going above a triple top or any fourth try to go beyond resistance is apt to be successful. Note that the count of four in Figure 42 is successful.

7. The old faithful price patterns are breakouts from long narrow congestion areas (island reversals, and head and shoulders reversals). However, these patterns do not appear often enough for most traders to wait and trade only these.

112

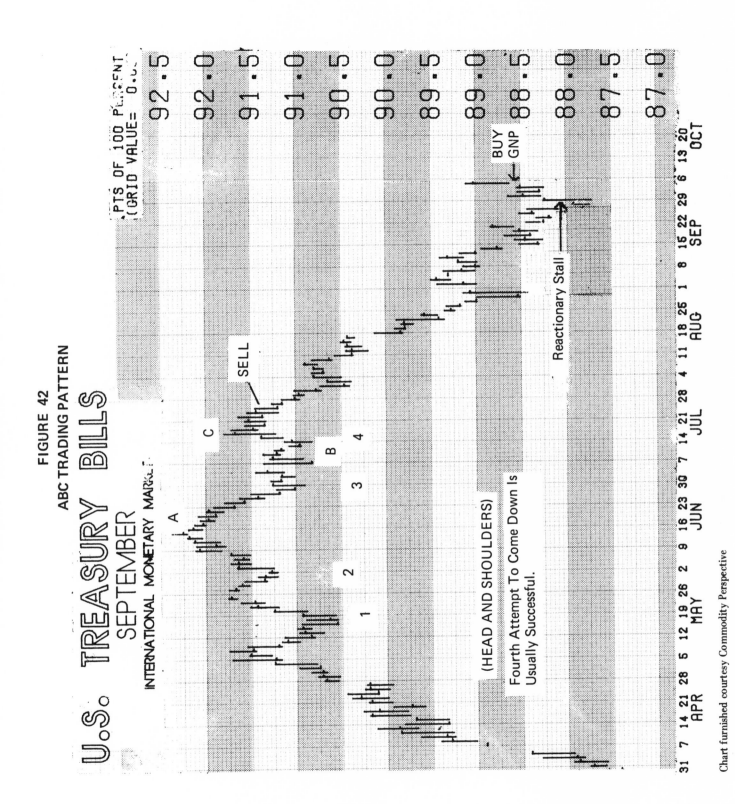

FIGURE 42

ABC TRADING PATTERN

U.S. TREASURY BILLS

SEPTEMBER

INTERNATIONAL MONETARY MARKET

PTS OF 100 PERCENT
(GRID VALUE = 0.0

92.5
92.0
91.5
91.0
90.5
90.0
89.5
89.0
88.5
88.0
87.5
87.0

BUY
GNP

Reactionary Stall

SELL

A

C

B

1   2   3   4

(HEAD AND SHOULDERS)

Fourth Attempt To Come Down Is
Usually Successful.

31 7 14 21 28 5 12 19 26 2 9 16 23 30 7 14 21 28 4 11 18 25 1 8 15 22 29 6 13 20
APR   MAY   JUN   JUL   AUG   SEP   OCT

Chart furnished courtesy Commodity Perspective

113

8. The reactionary stall is a good trade to take, as a rule. For example, if there is a sharp fast move down, then a close near a high of the day, this could be a snap back. This is a type of the pattern called "key reversal", where there is a long thrust day and close near the high along with high volume.

9. The complex stall is a variation from the reactionary stall above. Here the strongest member of a complex is watched for a stall out. If the stall holds for two days, a weaker month is shorted. Stalls have to be used with judgment, because people may be getting out before a report or for a long weekend. Commodities that are thin, and especially if they are used a lot by day traders, may not be good on a "stall" trade.

10. The "bounce-off" is another trade that should be used. When there are good resistance or support lines beyond the current price, if other indicators agree, and there is a price bounce. Go with this bounce for profits. Even if this trade proves to be wrong, it is usually a breakeven one, since you can get out when it comes back to the entrance price.

USING VOLUME AND OPEN INTEREST TO HELP ON ENTRY OR EXIT

1. Volume in markets with a lot of hedgers may be misleading. Those commodities having a lot of day traders will also give misleading indications of volume.

2. When there is about twice the normal volume, and open interest is down sharply, the hedgers are covering their shorts, expecting to be able to put them on higher (see Figure 43).

3. If there is about twice the normal volume and open interest is up sharply, the hedgers are selling; so expect this market to go down (see Figure 45).

ENTERING A RUNAWAY MARKET

1. Runaway markets usually only react for two days before continuing. Since so many people know this, it is generally necessary to enter on a one-

and-a-half day basis. If things are going extremely hot, there will only be a one-day pullback.

2. Another way to enter is by using the old "thrust" method, which was originated by Dunnigan. In a runaway down market, wait for a pullback, then put the stop buy just above the high of the down day. If the market goes down again, the stop buy is brought down to the high of this day before the opening of the next day. The stop buy orders are for each day only (see Figure 43). It is probably not a runaway market if price goes back many more days, but there should soon be a snapback of prices, resulting in a fill and profits; so keep the buy stop in before the opening each day.

ENTERING IN A CONGESTION AREA

1. This depends on whether or not the trade is to be long term or short. Reference here is for those wanting to get in for a longer trade.

2. Most wait to go in after a break from the bottom (or top).

3. On a fast leg, plan on the price going out of the congestion the way it came in. The best time to enter is near the middle of the congestion area, after the third spike has been made (see Figure 46). This is the same as buying an upturn in the third spike. If this is the first congestion after a sharp runaway leg, there may only be a two-spike congestion. The trader who has missed the move may want to go in on the turn of the second spike. Up flags, down flags, or triangles should be traded according to conventional methods of breakouts. The important thing is to be sure the directional indicators are pointed in the direction of a trade.

THE EASY ONES

Swings and channels are the easiest price patterns to enter. These have old lows or highs and trend lines from which to work. The thing to cause trouble may be some unexpected news item. Cycles, time and price balance points, rhythm count, and Elliott Wave count may be watched to give a more comfortable feeling about a trade.

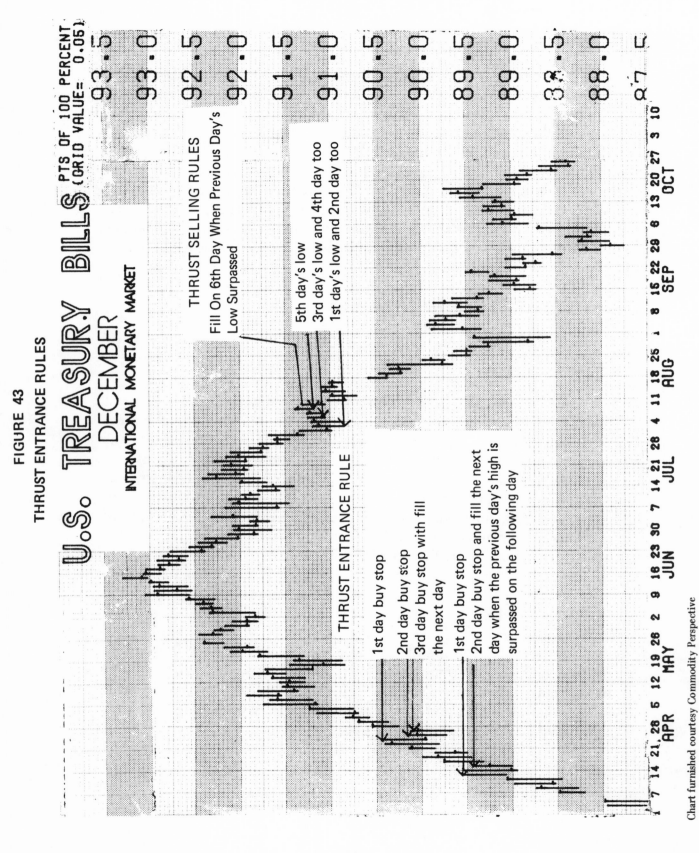

FIGURE 43
THRUST ENTRANCE RULES

U.S. TREASURY BILLS PTS OF 100 PERCENT
(GRID VALUE= 0.05)
DECEMBER
INTERNATIONAL MONETARY MARKET

THRUST SELLING RULES

Fill On 6th Day When Previous Day's
Low Surpassed

5th day's low
3rd day's low and 4th day too
1st day's low and 2nd day too

THRUST ENTRANCE RULE

1st day buy stop
2nd day buy stop
3rd day buy stop with fill
the next day

1st day buy stop
2nd day buy stop and fill the next
day when the previous day's high is
surpassed on the following day

Chart furnished courtesy Commodity Perspective

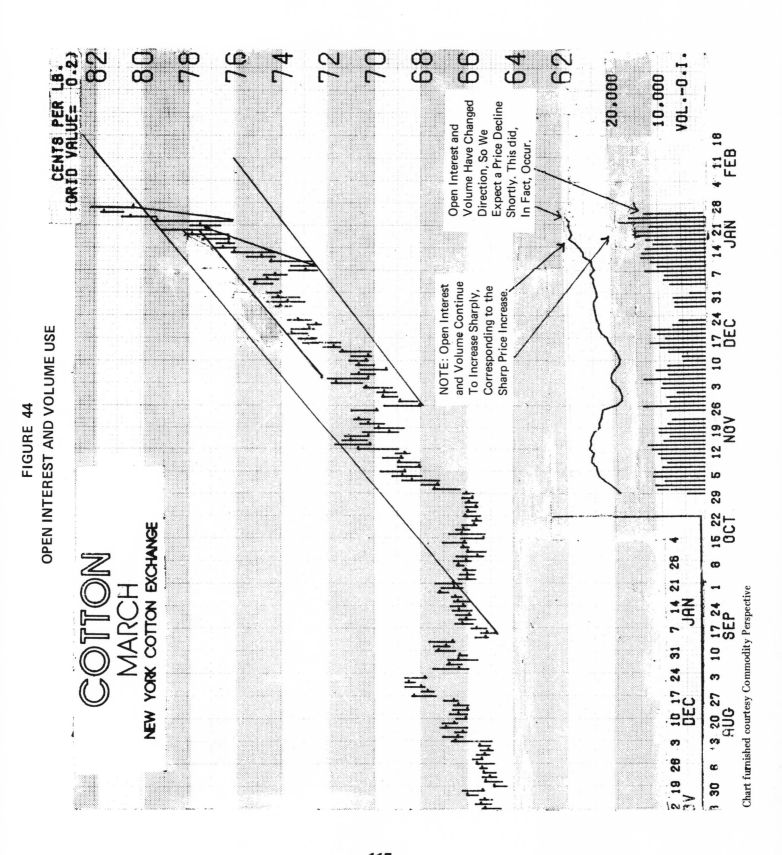

FIGURE 44
OPEN INTEREST AND VOLUME USE

NOTE: Open Interest and Volume Continue To Increase Sharply, Corresponding to the Sharp Price Increase.

Open Interest and Volume Have Changed Direction, So We Expect a Price Decline Shortly. This did, In Fact, Occur.

Chart furnished courtesy Commodity Perspective

117

FIGURE 45
OPEN INTEREST AND VOLUME EXAMPLE

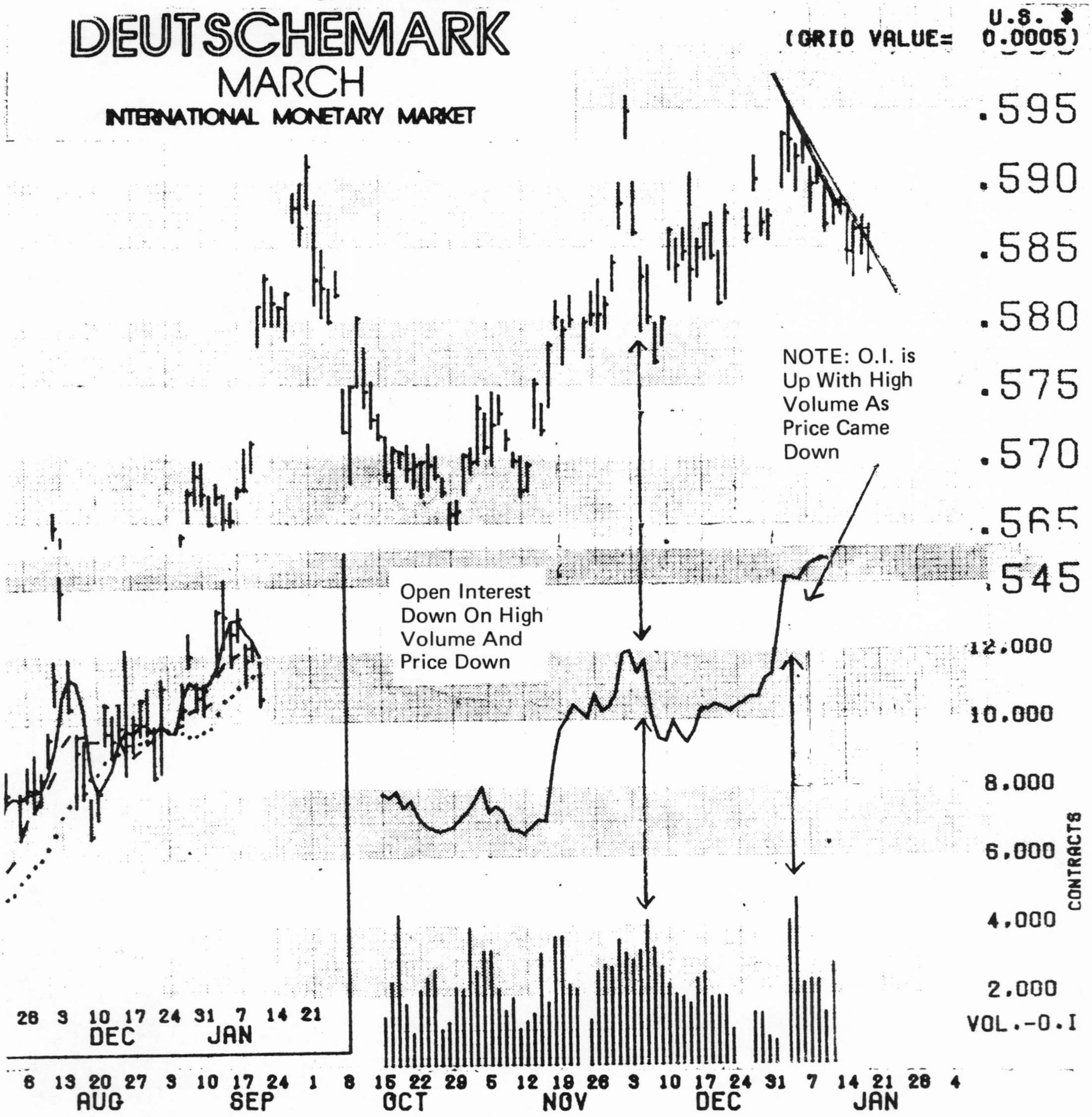

DEUTSCHEMARK
MARCH
INTERNATIONAL MONETARY MARKET

(GRID VALUE = 0.0005)   U.S. $

.595
.590
.585
.580
.575
.570
.565
.545

NOTE: O.I. is
Up With High
Volume As
Price Came
Down

Open Interest
Down On High
Volume And
Price Down

12,000
10,000
8,000
6,000
4,000
2,000
VOL.-O.I

CONTRACTS

26 3 10 17 24 31 7 14 21
DEC   JAN

6 13 20 27 3 10 17 24 1 8 15 22 29 5 12 19 26 3 10 17 24 31 7 14 21 28 4
AUG   SEP   OCT   NOV   DEC   JAN

Chart furnished courtesy Commodity Perspective

118

FIGURE 46
THREE SPIKES EXAMPLE

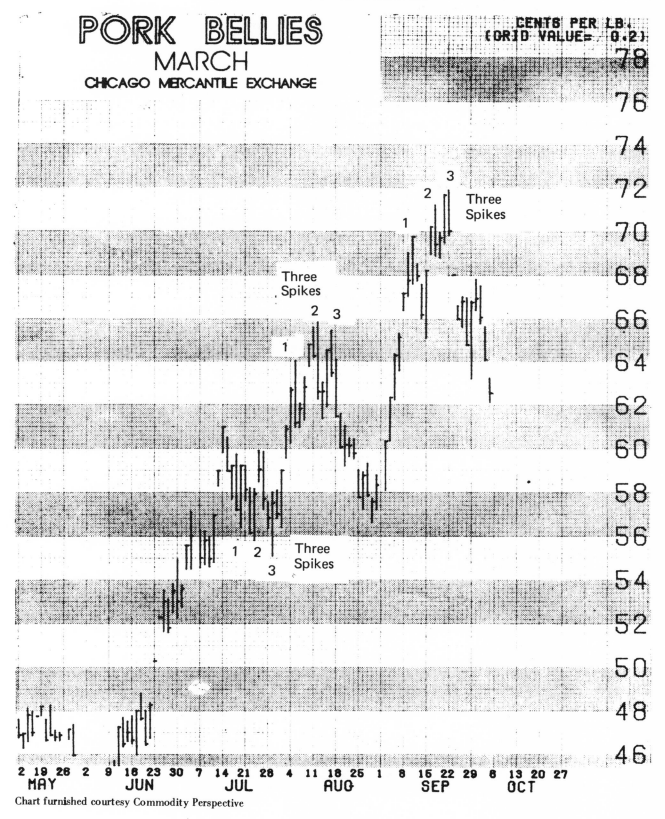

Chart furnished courtesy Commodity Perspective

TAKING PROFITS OR GETTING OUT

We believe in using sliding stops. When price approaches the Pivot Finder lines, it is a good time to move the stops closer. Price projection target areas should also have stops up closer. Where to get out depends on a trader. Long term traders who think they have reliable sources of fundamental information do not get out until their information indicates.

The best method of trading successfully on a longer term basis is by using the percent of commitment of traders applied to the open interest of back months, as mentioned earlier. If there is an extra large drop in open interest along with a decrease in the commitment of large traders, the hedgers are probably getting out. When there is an increase in the percentage of large traders plus a sharp rise in open interest, especially in the back months, the hedgers probably are going strong with this move.

CHAPTER 10

HIT THE TARGET

Many traders give little thought as to the destination of a trade. They try to let the market tell them when to get out. This is like shooting a gun without any object to hit. Young kids like to hear a gun pop, and novice traders get a strong urge to trade without proper consideration of the objective. It may be fun to just go sightseeing, but it is better to have something in mind as the reason for travel. Likewise, proper planning and knowing an estimated target is important before entering a trade.

Some books on commodities give vague instructions, such as to let the profits run and cut the losses short, but this is not enough. There need to be specific methods to determine a realistic target. This helps in money control and in picking the more worthy trades. It clarifies a trade and is a completion of the planning. A map or blueprint would be of little value without a completed object in mind. Proper planning for a trade should include price projection analysis.

TYPES OF PRICE PROJECTION METHODS

1. By using old highs or lows.
2. By some formula method, such as the zero sum.
3. Price pattern count or measurement.
4. Trendline or channel use.
5. Moving average crossings.
6. Cycle time methods.

NEW METHODS USED BY HAP TRADING TO HELP WITH PRICE PROJECTION

1. Using Pivot Finder lines.
2. Using recurring angle lines.
3. Using average angle lines and methods.
4. Using rhythm count.
5. Using time and price balancing.

PRICE PROJECTION OR TARGET ESTIMATION

1. Sharper angles should go further, because the move has more momentum behind it. Care must be taken not to use this in some choppy market or congestion area near a top or bottom where there may be accumulation or distribution. In the May Soybean chart (Figure 53) note that the angles became steeper and went further.

2. The channel width size should give the short term target. If this channel is crossed, it is expected to double. See Figure 13 of Chapter 2, "Pivot Finder Lines", which illustrates how price kept a channel width for five months.

3. Price going on an angle toward a Pivot Finder line gives a good target at the place where the angle of price line intersects the Pivot Finder line. Note in Figure 13 that a turn on these Pivot Finder lines usually meant a reversal.

4. Price going toward an old high or low line gives a price projection along with an estimated time. You not only know where it is going, but when it will get there because of the average angle rules.

5. Rhythm count can be used to verify time-price target estimations.

6. Use the cycle length to verify time-price projection.

7. The most exciting idea, however, is taking the known angle of travel along with the average length of a leg to estimate a target. (Use the average angle along with the average time found for a leg or move).

8. Use time-price balancing to predict a target.

    a. If price angle is too sharp, expect a sideways or choppy action to develop, so time and price can balance.

    b. If the price angle is too flat, expect price to turn up more sharply to balance with time.

c. When price and time are equal, expect a change.

9. Use Fib numbers to predict a target.

PRICE PROJECTION OR TARGET METHODS

1. Target by zero sum formula $(B + C) - A = T$.
2. Target by angle average and channel line.
3. Target by angle average with Pivot Finder lines.
4. Target by angle average with old high or low.
5. Target by angle average with average leg or swing.
6. Target by angle average with cycle time.
7. Target by angle average with time balance point.
8. Average three of these that are closest to each other. (The three nearest the same size).

FINDING THE TARGET WITH PIVOT FINDER LINES AND CYCLES

1. Using dividers (see Figure 48), it can be seen that Plywood was changing close to a one and one-fourth inch cycle length.

2. The pivot on April 30 and June 11 gave the angle for the lines going across. This line to a parallel from the bottom pivot on April 7 was also one and one-fourth inches apart; so we drew the top line on one and one-fourth inches, too.

3. The recurring down angle lines were put at one and one-fourth going across because this was the small cycle amount. So there is good symmetry with the down angles, up angles and across lines parallel apart.

4. A parallel across line was made off the top of May 20 and did fair at finding the top of July 21.

5. The up lines were on the average angle, over one and one-fourth inches on the across line to make them come out with the cycle length.

6. Thus Pivot Finder lines were made (plus the extra parallel line at the top). The down lines were on the same angle and same distance apart and the up lines were on the same angle and same distance apart. The across lines were parallel to each other and equal distances apart.

7. Stay in the market until the Pivo Finder lines are exceeded. Take profit when the Pivot Finder line is reached. If the target is reached early, take profits early and wait for the next crossing of a Pivot Finder line to reenter.

8. The objective was forecasted about three weeks in advance each time by seeing where the angle line would hit the Pivot Finder line.

USING TIME AND PRICE BALANCING TO PREDICT A TARGET

Time and price balancing to predict a target is shown in the illustrations on December Wheat (Figures 54 and 55).

In Figure 55, Wheat came down one hundred and five cents in fifty-five days, from February 4 to April 21. We did not expect it to do much for another fifty days, or to June 30. Sure enough, here is where it started up, went above resistance and eventually closed above resistance after the one hundred and five days. From this turning point on June 30, it went from a low of 445 to 490 in twenty-three days, making new highs on July 31. When it had churned sideways to down for twenty-two more days, balancing out this smaller time and price span, it started up again.

Now look at the second illustration of December Wheat (Figure 55). The previous chart on Figure 54 showed how price and time balancing can expect a change, and that price has a way of catching up with time when it gets twice the amount of time, or if time is more than price.

The bottom was confirmed at the failure of price at 423 on June 6, so new counting should begin from there, but the use of a forty-five degree angle line to help on these one-to-one charts must be started from the actual low. Parallels are drawn from the first main reaction up, and one is also drawn an equal distance from the main forty-five line. This proved to be the line that stopped price all the way to the top. The old high line at 523.50, made on February 4, 1980, was marked as a help in finding the target.

Price had come down one hundred and five cents and had squared itself. New count starting from here was marked off on the one hundred fifth day over, on November 3. This date should see time and price in balance. It developed that price did indeed come down sharply the next few days after November 3.

FIGURE 47
CHANNELS

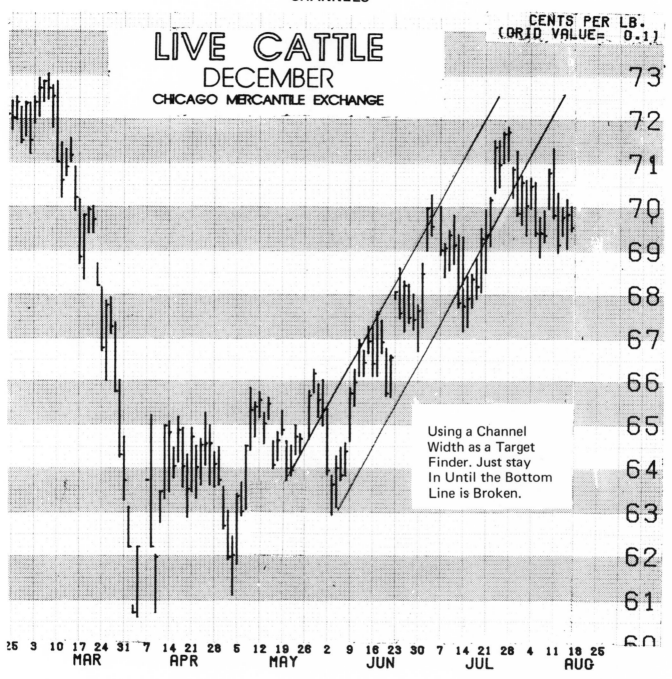

LIVE CATTLE
DECEMBER
CHICAGO MERCANTILE EXCHANGE

CENTS PER LB.
(GRID VALUE= 0.1)

Using a Channel
Width as a Target
Finder. Just stay
In Until the Bottom
Line is Broken.

Chart courtesy Commodity Perspective

125

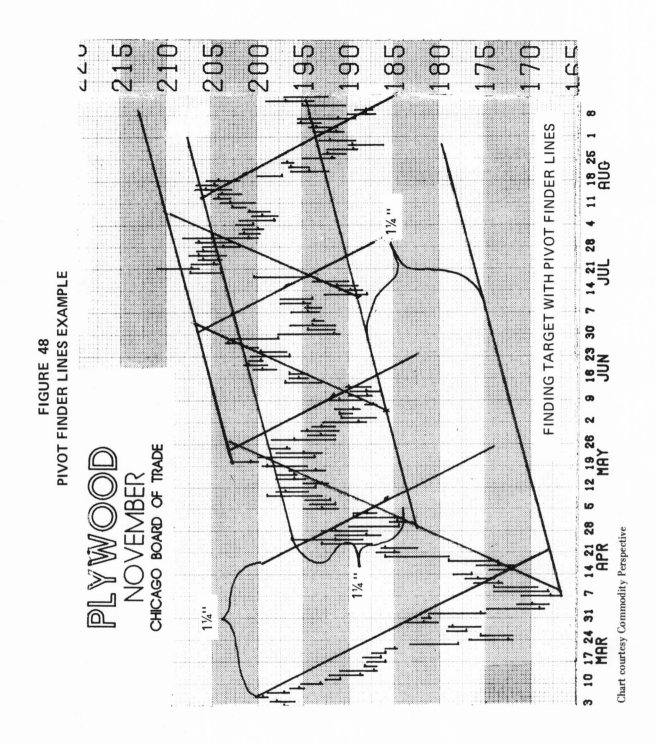

FIGURE 48
PIVOT FINDER LINES EXAMPLE

PLYWOOD
NOVEMBER
CHICAGO BOARD OF TRADE

FINDING TARGET WITH PIVOT FINDER LINES

1¼"

1¼"

1¼"

Chart courtesy Commodity Perspective

FIGURE 49
ANGLE AVERAGE LINE

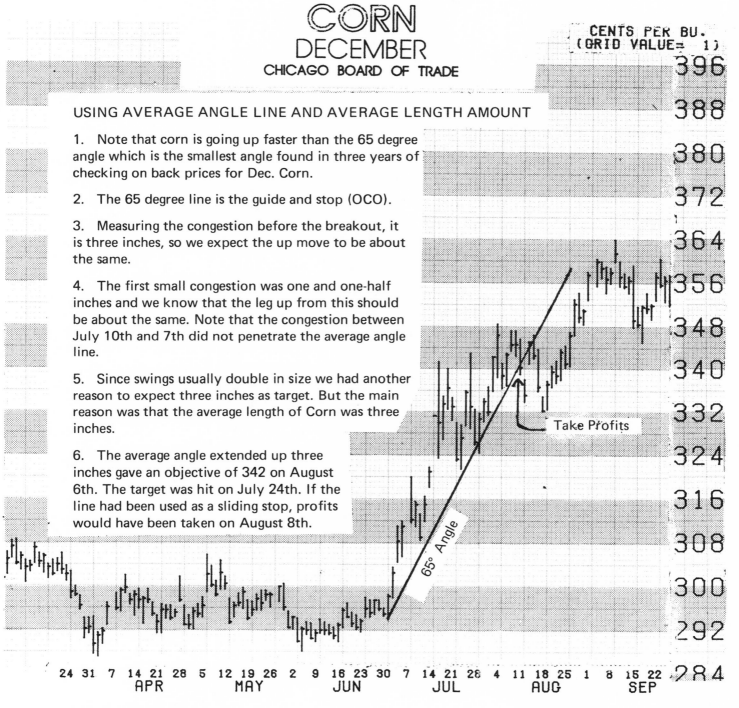

CORN
DECEMBER
CHICAGO BOARD OF TRADE

CENTS PER BU.
(GRID VALUE= 1)

USING AVERAGE ANGLE LINE AND AVERAGE LENGTH AMOUNT

1. Note that corn is going up faster than the 65 degree angle which is the smallest angle found in three years of checking on back prices for Dec. Corn.

2. The 65 degree line is the guide and stop (OCO).

3. Measuring the congestion before the breakout, it is three inches, so we expect the up move to be about the same.

4. The first small congestion was one and one-half inches and we know that the leg up from this should be about the same. Note that the congestion between July 10th and 7th did not penetrate the average angle line.

5. Since swings usually double in size we had another reason to expect three inches as target. But the main reason was that the average length of Corn was three inches.

6. The average angle extended up three inches gave an objective of 342 on August 6th. The target was hit on July 24th. If the line had been used as a sliding stop, profits would have been taken on August 8th.

Take Profits

65° Angle

24 31 7 14 21 28 5 12 19 26 2 9 16 23 30 7 14 21 28 4 11 18 25 1 8 15 22
APR   MAY   JUN   JUL   AUG   SEP

Chart courtesy Commodity Perspective

127

FIGURE 50

OLD HIGH LINE WITH AA LINES

USING OLD HIGH AND AVERAGE ANGLE FOR TARGET

1. Note that price had made a good bottom on April 1st, 19th and 30th.

2. Then price went up on the repetitious average angle. Since this was above forty five degrees and recurring, it seemed good.

3. The parallel average angle coming from the top of May 8th made equal distance pivot finder lines going up. This is action-reaction principles of equals and opposites.

4. The old high is extended out horizontally from the previous congestion area so it will be intersected with price as it proceeds up the average angle. This old high line will meet the average angle line on July 25th. But the objective was reached much early on July 2nd. A run up much quicker than expected is a warning to take profits.

5. It was not known on June 16th how things would turn out, but as long as price stayed above or to the left of the average angle line it is safe to stay in and wait for the target to be hit.

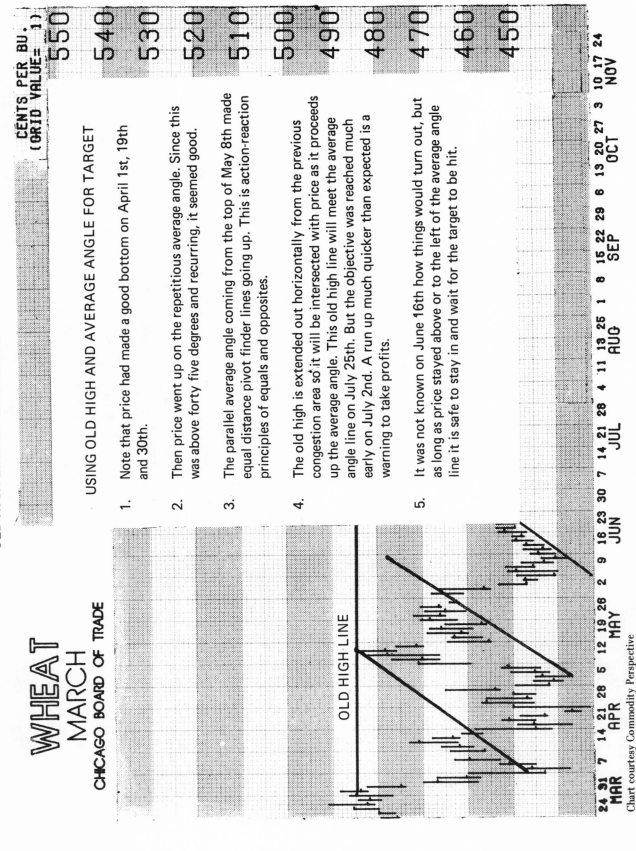

WHEAT
MARCH
CHICAGO BOARD OF TRADE

OLD HIGH LINE

CENTS PER BU.
(GRID VALUE= 1)

550 540 530 520 510 500 490 480 470 460 450

MAR APR MAY JUN JUL AUG SEP OCT NOV

128

FIGURE 51
OLD HIGH LINE AND ANGLE AVERAGE LINES

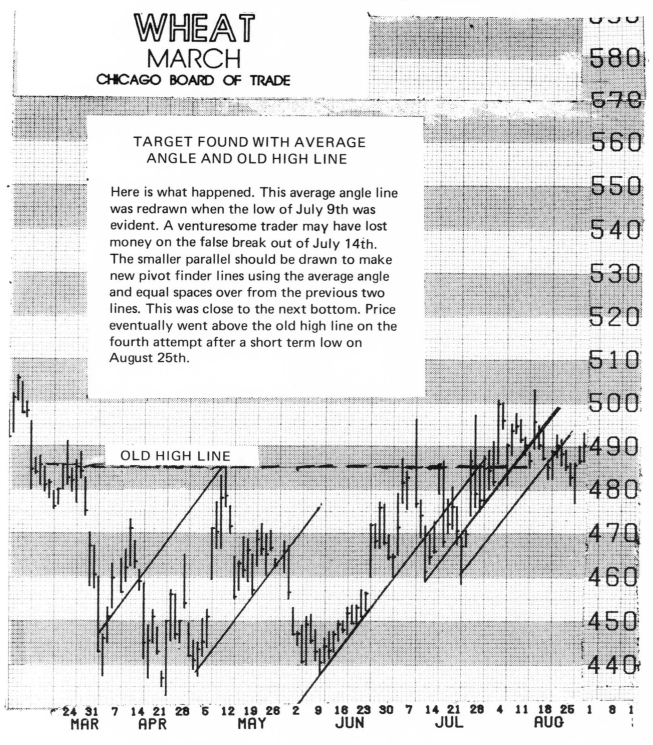

WHEAT
MARCH
CHICAGO BOARD OF TRADE

TARGET FOUND WITH AVERAGE ANGLE AND OLD HIGH LINE

Here is what happened. This average angle line was redrawn when the low of July 9th was evident. A venturesome trader may have lost money on the false break out of July 14th. The smaller parallel should be drawn to make new pivot finder lines using the average angle and equal spaces over from the previous two lines. This was close to the next bottom. Price eventually went above the old high line on the fourth attempt after a short term low on August 25th.

OLD HIGH LINE

Chart courtesy Commodity Perspective

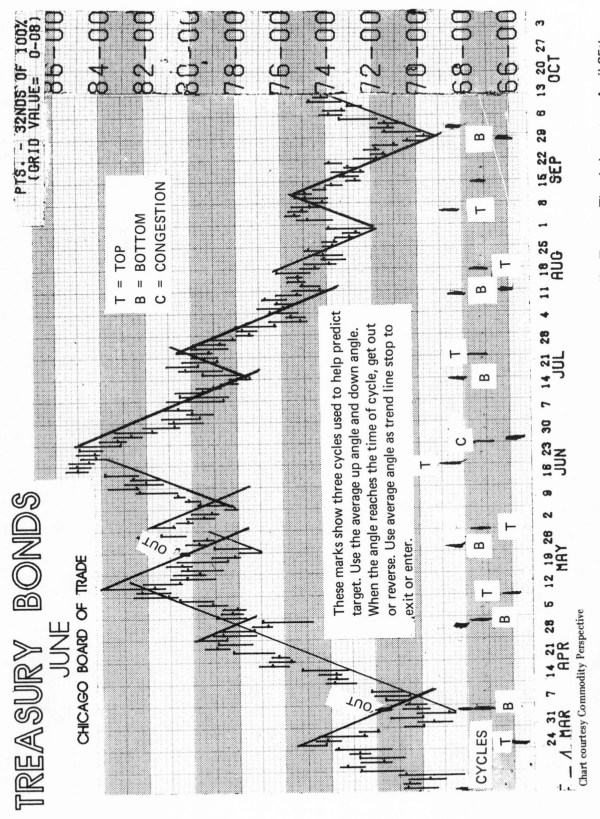

FIGURE 52

AVERAGE ANGLE LINES AND CYCLES

TREASURY BONDS
JUNE
CHICAGO BOARD OF TRADE

PTS. - 32NDS OF 100%.
(GRID VALUE = 0-08)

T = TOP
B = BOTTOM
C = CONGESTION

These marks show three cycles used to help predict target. Use the average up angle and down angle. When the angle reaches the time of cycle, get out or reverse. Use average angle as trend line stop to exit or enter.

This is an example of how cycles and average angles may be used to predict Targets. The shake-out on April 25th may have bothered some, but those trading more cautiously would have seen the potential bottom with two cycles close together on April 23rd and 25th and gotten out when price crossed the Average Angle line on April 23rd, then re-entered on April 28th when the down line was crossed. Enter or exit on the day the cycle is even with the Average Angle.

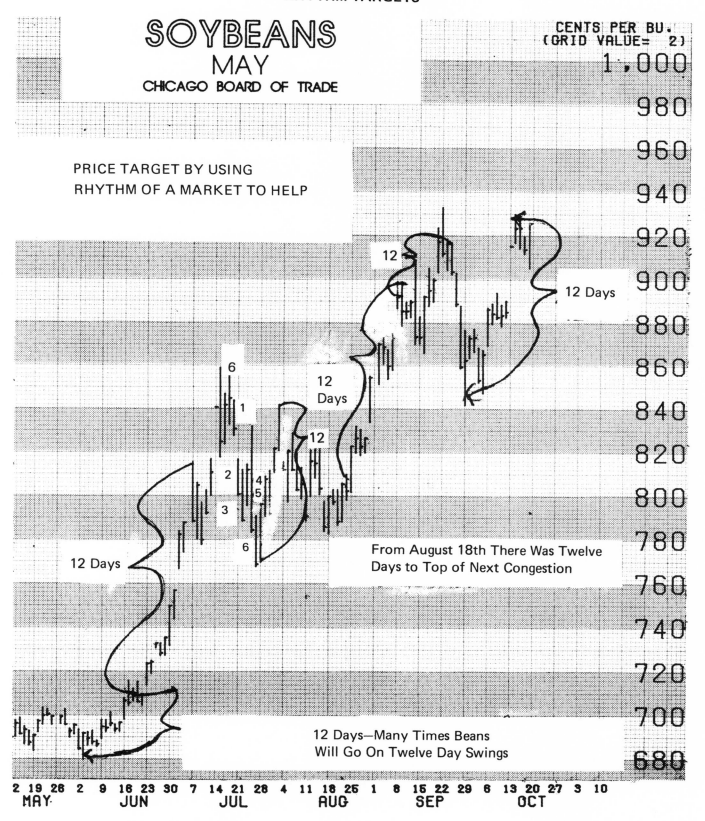

FIGURE 53
RHYTHM TARGETS

SOYBEANS
MAY
CHICAGO BOARD OF TRADE

CENTS PER BU.
(GRID VALUE= 2)

PRICE TARGET BY USING
RHYTHM OF A MARKET TO HELP

From August 18th There Was Twelve
Days to Top of Next Congestion

12 Days—Many Times Beans
Will Go On Twelve Day Swings

Chart furnished courtesy Commodity Perspective

131

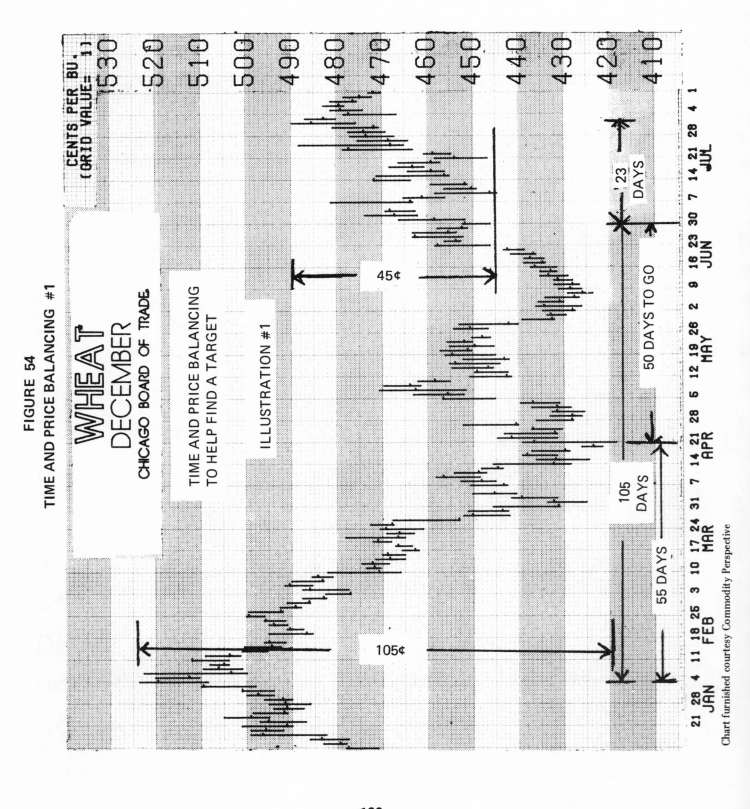

FIGURE 54
TIME AND PRICE BALANCING #1

WHEAT
DECEMBER
CHICAGO BOARD OF TRADE

TIME AND PRICE BALANCING
TO HELP FIND A TARGET

ILLUSTRATION #1

CENTS PER BU.
(GRID VALUE= 1)

45¢

105¢

23 DAYS

50 DAYS TO GO

105 DAYS

55 DAYS

132

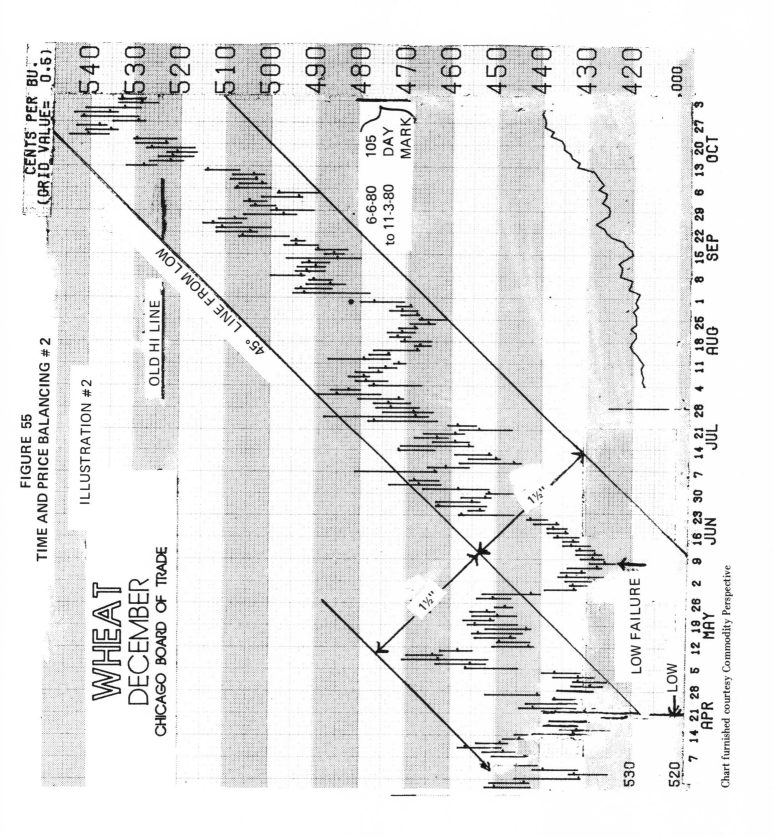

FIGURE 55
TIME AND PRICE BALANCING # 2

ILLUSTRATION #2

WHEAT
DECEMBER
CHICAGO BOARD OF TRADE

CENTS PER BU.
(GRID VALUE= 0.5)

OLD HI LINE

45° LINE FROM LOW

6-6-80
to 11-3-80

105
DAY
MARK

1½"

1½"

LOW FAILURE

LOW

Chart furnished courtesy Commodity Perspective

133

USING FIB NUMBERS TO HELP PREDICT A TARGET

Now take the Wheat chart (Figure 56) and count the Fib numbers on the days traded, starting with June 6. One, two or three days closings above a low is not enough for most people for confirmation of a low from which to go long; but when price closed above the low for five days, this is confirmation and the next Fib number count begins. Counting eight days from the fifth higher day (or on the thirteenth day from the bottom) there is a reaction, or small congestion area. Five days were counted first, then eight days. (The Fib ratio numbers are 1, 2, 3, 5, 8, 13, 21, 34, 55, 89, 144, etc.).

The reaction was three days, then it went up five days counting the day missed for a holiday. This also added up to twenty-one days from the bottom to the second reaction high. Thirty-four days came on the third reaction high and fifty-five days was on the low of the next reaction low. Eighty-nine days came on the third reaction low up from here. Fib ratio numbers add up and come out on change days of the market just too often to be coincidence. Fib ratio numbers do help in projecting market highs, lows, and reaction points.

USING THE ZERO SUM TARGET METHOD

Getting a target by using the zero sum method is like a friend once said, "It is good when it works." This method, reportedly first used by Dr. Ralph Heiser, is only good in an Elliott zig-zag price pattern. It shouldn't be used by itself, but it would be better than not having any target as is the practice with some traders. (See p. 106 of my first book, *Advanced Commodity Trading Techniques,* if you do not know this. B + C − A = T is the formula).

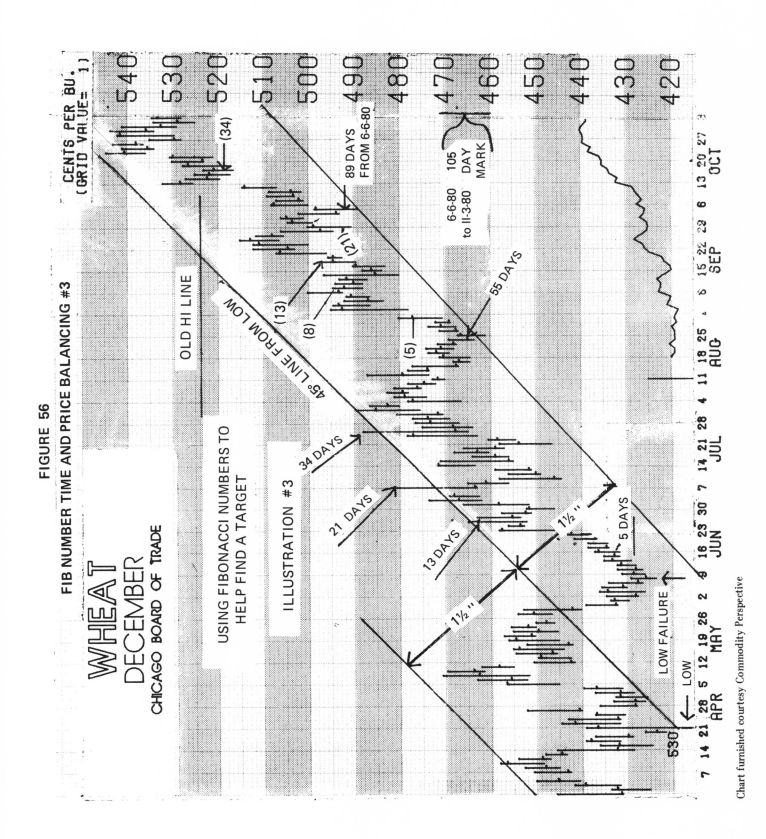

FIGURE 56

WHEAT
DECEMBER
CHICAGO BOARD OF TRADE

FIB NUMBER TIME AND PRICE BALANCING #3

CENTS PER BU.
(GRID VALUE= 1)

OLD HI LINE

45° LINE FROM LOW

USING FIBONACCI NUMBERS TO
HELP FIND A TARGET

ILLUSTRATION #3

(34)

89 DAYS
FROM 6-6-80

(21)

(13)

(8)

(5)

6-6-80
to 11-3-80

105
DAY
MARK

55 DAYS

34 DAYS

21 DAYS

13 DAYS

1½ "

5 DAYS

1½ "

LOW FAILURE

LOW

530

APR   MAY   JUN   JUL   AUG   SEP   OCT
7 14 21 28 5 12 19 26 2 9 16 23 30 7 14 21 28 4 11 18 25 8 15 22 29 6 13 20 27

540 530 520 510 500 490 480 470 460 450 440 430 420

Chart furnished courtesy Commodity Perspective

135

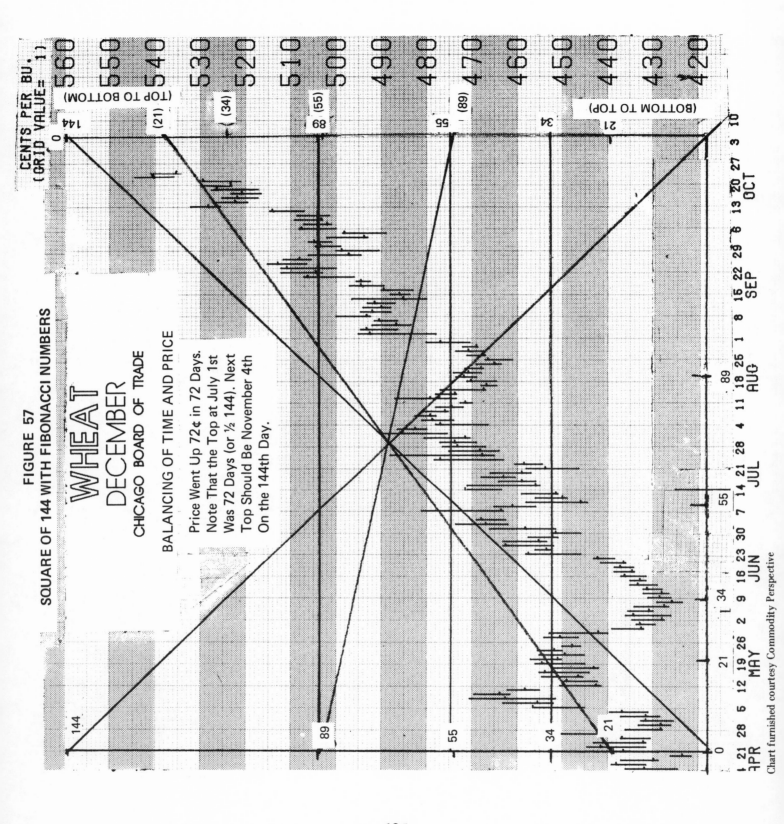

FIGURE 57
SQUARE OF 144 WITH FIBONACCI NUMBERS

WHEAT
DECEMBER
CHICAGO BOARD OF TRADE

BALANCING OF TIME AND PRICE

Price Went Up 72¢ in 72 Days.
Note That the Top at July 1st
Was 72 Days (or ½ 144). Next
Top Should Be November 4th
On the 144th Day.

CENTS PER BU.
(GRID VALUE = 1)

(TOP TO BOTTOM)

(BOTTOM TO TOP)

Chart furnished courtesy Commodity Perspective

CHAPTER 11

HOW TO PICK THE "HOT" TRADE

SELECTION CRITERIA

It is necessary to determine what is of primary importance and to follow a logical sequence of work. Decide what kind of trade is needed for a particular market, then study what type of market presently exists. Look at the big picture by way of weekly or monthly charts. Decide then whether or not this market is the kind and type you know how to trade. Never trade commodities until they have been studied enough for their characteristics and mannerisms to be known. A quick survey to learn what trades are coming up, and how each of these look, will help determine what risks are involved as well as what rewards are possible.

KIND OF MARKET

If the commodity is swinging wildly, be very cautious, especially if it has gone into a fast run that makes entry difficult. Check to see if the market is too dull or not moving enough to expect profits. Missing the first entry point makes it difficult to enter later. This could be chasing the market. What is the profit-to-risk ratio? How thin is this commodity? How about the volume and slippage factor? Before applying any selection index, these questions, and more, need to be answered.

TYPE OF TRADER

Every trader will develop a style that suits him best. He should not try to trade any other way. The length of trade, amount of actual risk capital, and whether or not a loss can be stood is only known by the trader. Few advisors can tell a trader what makes him uncomfortable. The size of a position depends on the risk capital available. The length of time to stay in a market depends upon the personal makeup of the individual and his personal problems of health or pressures of home or work. Some markets should be traded shorter than others, but there are markets for all traders. It is best for a trader to analyze himself and his circumstances thoroughly so he will know what he is capable of doing, both from a monetary standpoint and a "sleep-factor" viewpoint. While it is important to trade only a market that has been properly studied, it is especially important that the trader objectively evaluate his own emotional stability, family obligations, knowledge, and preferences.

TIME AVAILABLE

It is foolish for a trader to trade a market when he will not have time to do the necessary homework to determine how he is doing and where he stands. The way he trades depends on the time available for analysis and evaluation. He must know how long it takes to do the work on his charts and indicators and what criteria is necessary for staying in a market.

There is a story about a trader who lost a million dollars while having his portrait painted. Along with this story is a rumor that he committed suicide. Do not take the market lightly! Close out positions if there is not enough time to personally do the homework necessary. Do not let anyone persuade you to neglect a trading position. There are many safe short cuts in doing the homework. If it is taking more than ten hours a week, some analysis and education is needed to learn how to check a market more quickly, yet effectively.

MONEY MANAGEMENT PRINCIPLES

The kind of market to trade and the selection of a commodity position depends on money management techniques. We have a full section on this elsewhere, entitled "Keeping the Winnings." It must be kept in mind that the criteria and blue print made up for money management must be considered first, then the selection index can be used if needed.

TOOLS AND EQUIPMENT AVAILABLE

The time available and the portfolio to be chosen depend on a trader's tools. If he has a computer and can secure help to keep his routine work done, he can trade much more. It is said that W.D. Gann spent about $15,000 a year during the depression on office help and workers! Fifteen thousand dollars during the depression is easily worth over $150,000 today. Some think a big team with lots of expensive equipment is needed to beat the market. The helpers and the equipment will not perform any better than the trader who tells them what to do. There is a simple and efficient way to trade. Home computers are low priced and can do the work needed to analyze a small operation. A trader must keep his trades within his capabilities. He can trade the slower markets. He can test out indicators regularly on the computer or over back charts to determine how they are working and how reliable they are in various kinds of markets. A good rule to follow is to have the best tools available for what is to be done, but do not try to do anything beyond the capacity of the tools available.

THE OBJECT OF COMMODITY SELECTION

1. Eliminate poor trades so the 70 percent win-loss ratio can be improved. It should be better than this to win regularly year after year.
2. Know the amount to be risked and the potential for profit.
3. Pick trades in a proper framework of capital and time.
4. Evaluate the risk in terms of capital, time, and knowledge. Good selection will not help if only high risk trades are taken.

WHY DROP A WINNER?

The problem is not only finding a method that will work, but being able to work the plan. Traders often have a good method but the winning method can become boring and dull. To win, the trader must be able to keep himself doing what needs to be done. Few traders wait for the trade they really know. They get bored waiting for it to come around, then miss it by not keeping in touch with the market. This is why many people with good winning systems lose in the market. Trading is like an intricate machine, requiring constant vigilance and application. This is too much effort for some people. They beat themselves by not properly trading a winning system.

BEST MARKETS TO TRADE

This may sound facetious because any market that makes money is good. But there are some commodities with better odds of winning than others. Some commodities are occasionally controlled by a group of people—perhaps industry leaders or rich speculators. These markets are thin and more volatile. Large speculators make up a small percent of the market; but with enough money, they can trade thin markets—causing them to do unusual things which no indicator can predict. Unless a trader is experienced in handling these situations, knows when to trade them, and has enough money to withstand wider swings of the markets, he should pick the less spectacular market that is moving in a more orderly fashion. It is up to each trader to learn what markets he understands well enough to trade. Markets change frequently. The small trader must stick to those not jumping around so much. A desirable market should have a large volume and open interest for better executions; and not be influenced too much by foreign governments.

If in doubt about a market, ask the broker for a check on buyer participation. Only trade when commercials, small traders, and floor traders are all in a market. Sometimes the commercials will dominate and other times it will be the floor traders; but all three groups are important. Do not try to out-trade floor traders. They may be beaten for a while, but they will eventually learn how to win. Big commercials may lose money in the market but have this absorbed by profits in a cash product. They need to hedge with futures to lock in profits, so they can get financing and have stability in their operations. If the small trader is to win, he must learn how to trade with the commercials. Our study estimated about fifty-eight percent of the trades are for commercials, two percent for large speculators, twenty percent for floor traders and twenty percent for small speculators. Most of the time it is the floor trader who goes against the small speculator. The records show that, in the long run, small traders lose eighty percent of the time.

It is necessary to know who is making a market and how it operates. The "locals" will always fade the small trader, knowing from past experience that it pays. Learn how to trade with the commercials, for the markets are made for them. Without the commercials there would be no markets. Speculators help finance the commercials and they are needed. Locals are also necessary to keep liquidity in a market and furnish a place where futures can operate. All three are important and necessary.

The order of work and type of checklist required.
1. Kind and stage of market check list
2. Safest market check list
3. Rules for picking a market review
4. Price projection analysis
5. Commodity selection index

Note the above order of work to do. The market cannot be properly analyzed until a clear understanding is known regarding the stage, level and kind of market concerned. Each market should be traded differently. The cybernetic trading plan must possess the ability to change with each kind of market or it will lose. Most traders look at the big picture first by using weeklies for several previous years. The factors that influence a market are not only supply and demand, but also general economic conditions and interest rates.

Factors That Influence A Market
1. Money supply expanding or contracting.
2. Unemployment of country (high or low).
3. Balance of payments, good or bad?
4. Economy, escalating or deflating?
5. Interest rates, going up or down?
6. Dollar, gaining or losing against foreign currencies?
7. Inflation, increasing or decreasing?

The kind of market we will see is a result of such conditions. Some traders also watch weather forecasts and climate change predictions in their analysis of the market. The day trader, trying to get a little out of the market, may not think of these as important. But even the day trader needs to know the right trends of the market. Have a method of keeping these things in mind.

HAP'S HOT TRADES

In the strictest sense there are no sure-thing commodity trades, but some trades have a much better chance of winning and are called "sure-thing" trades. A better word is HAP's hot trades. A safer trade has the following characteristics:
1. Your indicators have tested well in these markets.
2. It is an orderly market, not jerking or jumping too much.
3. It has good trader participation, with all three kinds of traders represented.
4. It has liquidity, with sufficient volume and open interest.
5. It is not subject to a known pending political action.
6. The weather picture is not dangerous. For example, never short orange juice in January when a freeze scare may hit Florida (if you want to play a safer market).
7. The margin is reasonable or within capability. High margins must be considered for calculating rate of return.
8. The entrance ability is within loss factor capabilities. Stops should be put where floor traders are not apt to get them. If the stop cannot be placed safely, within the money loss boundaries of a trader, he should pass on the trade.

9. The safe trades are generally those that can be seen approaching for some time and have been tracked on weeklies first.

10. A high percentage of the indicators have a favorable signal for the trade.

RULES FOR PICKING A MARKET TO TRADE

1. Has this commodity been thoroughly studied?

2. Are the previous patterns in its history, under similar circumstances, known to the trader?

3. Is the present price pattern one of previous success when it has been traded?

4. Is the market too volatile for money on hand?

5. Will this trade be within the boundaries of conservative money management rules?

6. Are there any pending family or business activities that might interfere?

7. What time is available to devote to this trade? (Have a definite time and place.)

FINDING THE TARGET

Our main work on price projection analysis is found in Chapter 10, entitled "Hit the Target." Here is a list of the types of work done there. Work each for the trade and put the results on a duplicate of this list.

Determine Target
1. By the Zero sum formula $(B + C) - A = T$
2. By angle comparison
3. By angle average with channel line
4. By A.A. and Pivot Finder line

5. By A.A. with old high or low line
6. By A.A. with average leg or swing
7. By A.A. with cycle time
8. By A.A. with time and price balance point
9. Average of three closest targets found by above methods to locate true target.

COMMODITY SELECTION INDEX EXAMPLE

1. Results check list	40%
2. Commercial participation	25%
(See Accumulation/Dist. section)	
3. Margin Requirements	5%
4. Win-loss ratio at least three-to-one	10%
5. Relative strength composite index	10%
6. HAP price reversal index	10%

CHECK LIST RESULTS

1. Economy check list
2. Safe trade check list
3. Picking a market check list
4. Money control check list
5. Win-loss ratio results more than 2 to 1
6. Commodity selection index

CHAPTER 12

KEEPING THE WINNINGS

WHY A 70% WIN-LOSS RATIO STILL NEEDS MONEY CONTROL

To some traders it probably seems strange to hear an advisor boast about his win-loss ratio, then later tell about his good money management methods. Why does a person with a seventy percent win-loss ratio need to be concerned about money control? The problem is the expenses involved with trading, plus the chance that the trader can get caught in some fiasco, such as the grain embargo by the President. Sudden and unexpected weather conditions, political changes or national disasters may cause a loss. In addition to these unexpected events that may take away the profits, there is also the daily expense of the office, commissions to brokers and slippage in the execution of a trade. Any combination of these can cause a winning system to lose money unless care is taken.

WHAT TO DO ABOUT IT

The first way to make the bottom line better is to have a good commodity selection index, and only trade when the odds are better than average. If trading techniques are good, and only the best trades taken, the win-loss ratio should improve to about 85 percent. With the necessary expenses subtracted out of this, a trader has a good chance of putting money in the bank each year.

Before any trading is done, the trading technique should be traded on paper, or tested on back prices, using exacting rules, to get a realistic appraisal of what it may do in various kinds of markets. The selection method should also be tested over at least three years of back data under various conditions.

RISK CONTROL FACTORS

1. Have good price projection techniques and take only trades that show a three-to-one return potential.

2. Risk no more than five percent per contract traded and limit the total risk at one time to thirty percent of capital.

3. Diversify a portfolio with representative markets and commodities.

4. If there is only $10,000.00 capital for the present volatile markets, mini-contracts can help diversify. There must be enough money to ride out a string of losses, or failure is certain.

5. Do not trade thin markets unless special research is personally done to recognize the right situation. Trading must always be done under the most favorable conditions.

6. Use stops wisely. Generally, on-close-only stops are best.

THE CONSERVATIVE APPROACH

1. Trade with the trend.
2. Do not try to pick tops or bottoms.
3. Stay out of the market in front of major reports.
4. If in doubt, stay out.
5. Seldom pyramid.

With all these things going for us, how can we lose? Remember Murphy's Law? It is certainly possible. In fact, regardless of the best preparation, most traders will lose. Why? Because this is a physical matter as well as an intellectual one. Knowing all the rules on how to play does not make someone a winner at golf. The same thing is true in trading. **It takes good health and strong determination to be able to stick to a plan and execute it properly.**

LEARN TO SAY "NO"

When it becomes known that you are a trader, every huckster in the country will be trying to convince you that he has the best advice to sell or some methods you just cannot afford to be without. There are about 100,000 traders in the United States, but there must be 300,000 salesmen. Advisors, chart salesmen, weather predictors, and specialty men all hope to make money off the trader. There will be constant phone calls with "sure fire methods." Those who can talk you into telling them what you are doing, will try to tell you to do something different. Friends and kin who learn of your activities will offer unsolicited advice. At times, scare tactics will be used to try to get you into (or out of) a position. Rumors will be circulated to shake your faith. Touters will be touting from all directions, using what prestige and conviction they can muster, to sell their story. Big money interests are very adroit at getting press releases to help their cause. Every effort will be made to play on emotions of fear or greed in order to trap traders into making mistakes.

You will learn the difference between being a student of war and going into battle. The trading field is a battle of wits and nerve, being played for big stakes. Those who survive with money made every year must use iron discipline. A psychologist friend once said, "Just stand in the corner and practice saying 'No' every morning so you will be ready for the salesmen."

147

THE SECRET FORMULA

Another obstacle to making the 85 percent plan bring home money can be the trading method or system. Many people buy their trading plan. These plans may work well until too many people begin to use them, then they become a factor in the market. A trading plan must be limited to principles that are sound and basic. The combinations of use, and order of use, of the basic theory must be known only to you. Big computers are going every day, trying to determine what procedures are most in use and what is the best way for their owners to make money. The basic theory behind the trading plans are few, but the combinations of use and techniques are many. It is possible for big computers to analyze markets and tell much about what is in use. Most market analysts have attended the same kind of schools and come up with a lot of the same answers. The good trading plan of today may not be as good next year. Too many people may be doing the same thing. Many people do not realize the actual mathematical formula behind their plan and do not know how similar it can be to something they think is different. For example, some people do not know that angle trading and momentum are based on the same math principles. So it is vital to not only have a secret trading plan, but to also keep testing and researching to know how to change it at a future date when it begins to lose its value.

It is imperative to have a trading plan known only to you and not listen to anyone who may try to influence you. Also change your methods occasionally. To keep the world away from your trading procedure may take drastic measures, but it is necessary. These are days of team efforts with computer men and other staff help, but they must be loyal and accept your leadership.

On testing, the main thing is to be objective and give the benefit of the doubt to the loss rather than to the win. Proper slippage must be included, and all kinds of markets must be tested. It is important to know which works best for your plan. The way of testing will depend on the kind of plan used. Some testing can be done by going over old price charts. The author has spent many tedious hours checking on various aspects of the market for trading plans.

148

FIVE MISTAKES THAT CAUSE TRADERS TO LOSE

1. The most common mistake is not having a broad enough perspective to know what things come first and what is most important. Many times a trader will be trying to learn something that is not important at a particular stage of the market. How to trade the market changes with each level of the market and each section of a campaign. If the bulls are in control, there is typical maneuvering expected from them. This changes as progress is made. The trader must first understand what stage the market is in and recognize the kind of market unfolding.

2. This is similar to the mistake of trading one kind of market the same as another. Everyone know what happens when a trending market starts chopping. Most traders now have methods for detecting the two main kinds of markets. But do they realize that the price level makes a difference too? A choppy market at the bottom must be viewed differently than a choppy market at the top. Then there are swinging markets and labored move markets that are to be considered. Each of these must be treated differently at various levels of price or stages of progress in the campaign.

3. Know what kind of indicators to use on these various kinds and stages of a market. It takes knowledge and experience to know the right techniques to use at the right time.

4. Not doing your own work is another big mistake. There is no free ride. Those who offer to do your analysis or who offer free advice must be refused. There may be some information someone may give that will help with your analysis, but the way this is applied must be your way. Everyone does things differently and you must use your own methods so you will really understand all the implications.

Not knowing the proper relationship of values, not knowing what is most important, and not having the right perspective is covered above; and now we will consider failure to do what should be done.

5. This mistake usually comes from getting bored. There is often some dull work that must be done while trading. Traders must do the homework necessary to trade properly. Those who get bored, or for some reason fail to get their homework done, are tempted to take a shot at something—in hopes that they may be hitting the right thing. They will be tempted to ask

149

the broker or someone else what to do. There will be overtrading, and eventually they will experience a lot of losses, because proper care was not taken to work the plan as it was meant to be worked.

Some traders like to think they are doing their own trading when they play their hunches. These say they do not want a mechanical plan, but they are just kidding themselves. All they want is the fun involved, like a crap-shooter, and are too lazy or too bored with the dull routine necessary to do what must be done to win. The difference between the winner and the loser is usually in attitude. The winner is willing to do the things necessary to win, whereas the loser is not. There are simple methods that can be used to win in the market, but they are not all exciting. Most produce no intellectual satisfaction. It is a matter of grinding out the trades and putting them on.

FOUR REASONS MOST TRADERS DO NOT MAKE MONEY

1. The main reason most traders do not realize profits is that they do not have a strong desire to make money. They want the ego satisfaction of beating the market, or the thrill of playing the game, but making money is not the most important thing with them. A winner must be very competitive—like a cannibal that goes after money. He does what he has to do to survive, knowing that there are other cannibals out there after him. He is like the hunter out for the kill. Intense desire and concentration is required to outsmart the quarry and bring home the bucks.

2. The second reason for failure is the subjective personal attitude of many traders. This type wants to prove to his wife or someone else how smart he is, then when he takes a loss, it hurts too much. He does not have the ability to go through the rough and harsh reality of the market without letting his feelings cause him damage. Emotion usually clogs good channels of reasoning. The good trader does his work in a relaxed manner, without becoming so involved personally that his plan of operation is disrupted. A certain amount of fear or concern is needed, along with a certain amount of greed, to keep the trader alert and striving to win; but too much

150

emotional stress will soon wear him out and cause him to perform poorly. The trader must be like the battle trained gunner who has learned, through hours of practice, to do things routinely and methodically, following his plan and methods without change or mistake. The old pro knows that there will be times of bad luck and learns to triumph in spite of adversity.

3. Another common reason for failure is lack of timing. Knowing when not to trade is as important as knowing when to trade. If a trader misses a good trade, then, in urgency or annoyance at himself for having missed out, he goes into lesser trades, the odds will eventually be tipped against him (by taking more mediocre trades then good ones). Timing can be affected by the personal life of the trader, too. If he has a family, they must understand his passion for winning and be sympathetic with him. One trader said that the good trader should be single, to not have any interference from a family.

4. The last main reason for failure is not having the proper goals set for winning. Some traders try to achieve too much too fast. When they win, they are not satisfied and feel they should have won more. Worthy and realistic goals must be set. The plunger may win today and lose tomorrow, but he will eventually end up broke, unless he happens to be in the small one percent of those who are extremely lucky. The problem with the plunger is he does not know when to quit. Instead of banking half or more of his winnings, he just keeps going up and down like a yo-yo, as long as he has enough to be in the market.

The trading method should be able to predict expected profits. Trade as safely as possible and plan to come out with a reasonable profit, as in any other business. Realize the chance for the "plunger in the market" to win is no better than in any other situation where excess risks are taken. Plungers become losers. Be willing to perform the work and routine necessary to make better than average trades, but have no illusions about getting rich quick. Know that if the risk is great, you may win a lot; but the odds are more in your favor if you will follow a conservative trading plan.

TEACHINGS THAT NEED REVIEWING

There are some things about the market that are taught as a general rule, or were taught in earlier years, that may not be true now. New computer and electronic inventions have brought about changes. With quoting machines and microcomputers in the price range of small traders, they are learning to trade with much more skill and ability. The large traders also are using computers to a much greater extent. Much more training material is available to the small trader. There are a number of significant improvements in technical methods that are now known by traders.

With inflationary conditions of the times, there are many more commodity traders and the markets have taken on new characteristics. New possibilities need to be considered by the trader. Since each commodity has certain characteristics under the various conditions, the way to trade each should be different.

Following are some ideas that are not necessarily advocated by the author, but they are offered for study as worthy possibilities. Things are changing. These methods may be worthy of your investigation.

1. Averaging down—By the old school of thought, this generally has been considered to be bad, but can be good if done under the proper circumstances. One good time for its use is when a number of contracts are to be accumulated in a specified price range. When price gets to the top of that price range, the trader needs to start accumulating on the proper percent, according to how much he wants to acquire. If his work says buy in a price range, it does not matter if he buys on the way down or the way up. In fact, near the top of the price range may be the only place he can get filled. Others may be doing the same thing in the same place and forcing the market up, so that the lower limits may never be reached on this move. An average down basis is also useful for acquiring contracts when price goes to near contract lows, or better, to historical lows. The well funded trader may acquire contracts here, knowing that he can take delivery if necessary. The commodity must be storable, and it pays to know in advance what costs are involved for storage in case this is done. Averaging down near historic lows should be done so that there will not be much loss

from waiting out a bad position. The price does have a limit on how far it can go down. People with the money to store commodities and hold them can trade differently than those who do not. The rules applying here are having enough money, price being at low levels, and knowing that the economic conditions are favorable for the rise of this commodity in the not too distant future.

2. The next big category that needs to be examined is day trading, or short term trading. For most people this is probably a no-no; but for others who can find the time and have the money to get the right equipment, this may be the way to make money. We know of more and more traders getting a quote machine and computer to do short term trading.

One reason the short term trader may succeed where the long term one may not, is due to the longer term traders' use of computers. The small trader with simpler methods at hand can see the excess runs by computer technicians handling large managed accounts, and can take advantage of this knowledge to make money. Another reason is the ability of the short term trader to trade the congestion areas, which is a hard thing for the big traders to do. They have non-trending techniques, but these do not change as quickly from one system to the next as can be done by the small trader. If the small trader knows his work, he can take advantage of the inadequacies found in the big managed accounts.

3. The other technique that needs to be considered by some is the one called the "Martingale Method." This is the old theory of runs or games, where one doubles up everytime he loses until he wins, then he drops back to one contract and starts again. Articles have come out by noteworthy analysts from time to time about using this technique. One such article was by Robert O. Pelletier, called *"Money Management for Martingale Commodity Traders"*, which came out in the Commodity Journal in 1973. It was said in this article that a Martingale scheme could be applied safely. Whether or not this was a good technique is not known. Hope has been raised about this method for some by the games offered on microcomputers, where one can always beat an opponent by using this method unless the opponent also uses it. The theory of runs is explained on page 267 of Kaufman's, *"Technical Systems and Methods."* More and more this question is coming up. This way of trading is definitely for the well funded. The smaller trader may try something like this on mini-

contracts if he has a method that is doing at least 50 percent right, and if he has over ten times the margin needed to trade the maximum amount of contracts he plans to trade. Assuming the doubled amount to run at 1, 2, 4, 8, 16, he would need sixteen times the margin for thirty-one mini contracts, or about $300,000. If he had a system that consistently did not lose less than four times in a row, then he may be venturesome enough to try this. It is not conservative trading, but it is something to think about and research further. There are usually larger skids on mini-contracts, and having a seat on the mid-America Exchange would be of great help. If day trading with a seat on the Exchange, the margin would be much smaller.

CHAPTER 13

ANGLE AVERAGING TRADING

It has been proven that at least eighty percent of those who evaluate trading are wrong. The reasons they have for entering the market are incorrect. From this concept grew the Bullish Concensus of Opinion method of trading.

Knowing that most people are wrong gives an opportunity for profits by taking advantage of the excesses caused by those using improper methods, which drive price out of line. All that is necessary is to be able to detect when prices are out of line. Detecting price out of line with how it should be can be seen by learning the average angle, average length of a swing of a commodity, and the average time in these average swings. With the average swing length, the amplitude of a move is obtained. The angle gives the velocity of the swing, and the time in the swing shows the volatility of the commodity. Knowing the time a market has to go, the volatility, velocity and amplitude is all one needs to be able to make money in the market. The average of these represents what most people are thinking. When price goes away from the average, odds are in favor of some profits since price is out of line with how it should be normally.

BACK WORK NECESSARY

This method is based upon back work that must be done to find the

155

average time and average recurring angle for each leg of the market according to the level of price and stage of the market. This research, for those who are serious about the market, consists of taking the same month of a commodity back three years. It is most helpful if you have a computer on which to test back data. On grains, it is best to use a new crop month, such as May. Find the average time in each leg and each reaction. Then find the recurring angle for up angles and down angles.

The illustration on Figure 58 shows how Pivot Finder lines may be used to find the average angles and their distances apart. Note that going across the page, price changed or had a congestion five times on equal time periods, and price had the same length leg or swing four times. Learn to use Pivot Finder lines. Average angle lines are not equal spaces apart and would conform closer to the price pattern, but PFL's do help in locating the right angle and length of a swing.

In case someone may think this is too much trouble for what it is worth, we wish to say, ahead of complete explanation, that knowing what the angle is and the time spent in travel gives the ability to estimate price moves by using a math formula. Doesn't this stimulate interest? With some tedious homework, there comes the ability to be able to estimate how far a move should go.

If the average time for a move is known, this can be compared with the progress of a current move to see if it is slow or fast. The same holds for the average pitch or degree of angle for a commodity. If the commodity is not on the average angle, this is a way to estimate how far it is off; and how slow or fast the expected target is approaching.

THEORY USED

1. Momentum (by comparing angle degree)
2. Price projection or target analysis
3. Recurring angles, swings, and channels
4. Cycles
5. Time-price balancing (see Figure 59)
6. Reversal rules

156

FIGURE 58
P F LINES # 1

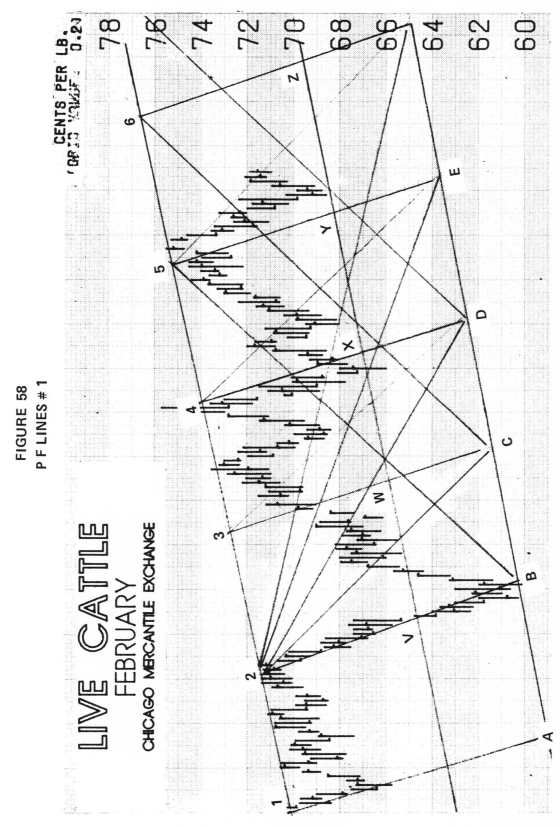

LIVE CATTLE
FEBRUARY
CHICAGO MERCANTILE EXCHANGE

CENTS PER LB.

Chart furnished courtesy Commodity Perspective

157

FIGURE 59
P F LINES # 2

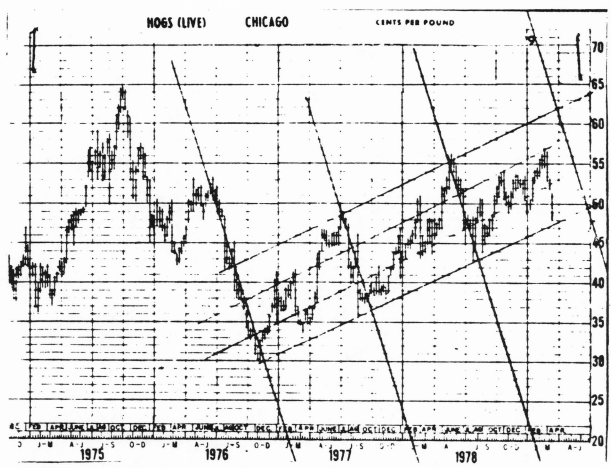

Chart furnished courtesy Commodity Research Bureau

BASIC ASSUMPTIONS

1. With the average or repetitious angles found, when an angle goes off one average, it is assumed that another repetitious angle will be used.

2. The steepness of an angle gives the momentum of price.

3. With more momentum (or a steeper angle) the price should go further. With a flat angle (and less momentum), price should not go as far.

4. The forty-five degree angle is considered middle in an up market, since it is half-way between the highest and lowest degrees capable of being used. Price cannot go up on more than a ninety degree angle as this would make it going backwards; and if it gets below the horizontal line, it is not going up but down; so the forty-five degree angle is in the middle. Care must be taken to make sure that the commodity is charted on a one to one scale, or the forty-five degrees will not be correct with price.

5. In going over the back price for estimating the average up angle and average down angle, the same price scale must be used for all the charts. Weeklies will be all right for long term trading if dailies are used for entrance confirmation.

6. For a quick check on the status of a market, if the amount of the average up-angle is more than forty-five degrees, this denotes strength. Should it be less than forty-five degrees, this roughly denotes weakness.

7. The down market should travel below a fifty-five degree angle, as price goes down faster than it goes up for most commodities. The amount the average down-angle is above or below the fifty-five degree angle indicates whether or not the market normally is slower or faster in its down moves. Each commodity has its own characteristics and they all must be analyzed and understood.

REPEATING CHANNELS

Just as there are repeating angles, there are recurring channels. There should be an average channel size for each season of the year. If some time is spent going back over the three-year charts, it will be found that the channels for small size swings will be about the same width each year unless some unusual situation occurs. There is a recurring small size channel width—as well as angle—that should be found and known to the trader.

WHEN AVERAGE ANGLES SHOULD WORK BEST

The average angle is only found in swings or legs of the market and not in congestion or in choppy areas. Since this is true, it follows that one should not try to find an average angle in a narrow choppy market or congestion area. These can be eliminated as they become known. Markets like the labored move that goes in a channel should have a recurring angle. Examples of these can be seen in Figures 60-63. If possible, avoid tops or bottoms in picking the best times to use average angles. Action in these areas is often not normal, especially in tops where there may be hectic swings. This may be true for some bottoms too, because those accumulating large positions sometimes cause spikes in market action. Fast run ups on bottoms often mean a retreat back to congestion or even to the main base line. The time to expect average angles is when price goes out of congestion areas, triangles, or some choppy sideways area of the market.

SHORT CYCLE AVERAGE

The next study is to find the current average size of angles, swings, and channels occurring in the short cycle time period of the commodity. This is to define boundaries for making comparisons. With this information obtained, it is possible to compare the average angle of the short cycle of the present option with that of the main averages. This gives valuable reference points from which to work in estimating moves and price direction. This information should be obtained by going back five or six months, using the short cycle time period. The following paragraphs explain how this is done.

HOW TO MAKE COMPARISONS

1. Make angle comparisons between the short cycle time periods and the main angles, as averaged over back price, to see if the current angles are different. Use only legs or swings for angle comparisons. Note the graph

FIGURE 60
BEANS REPEATING CHANNELS

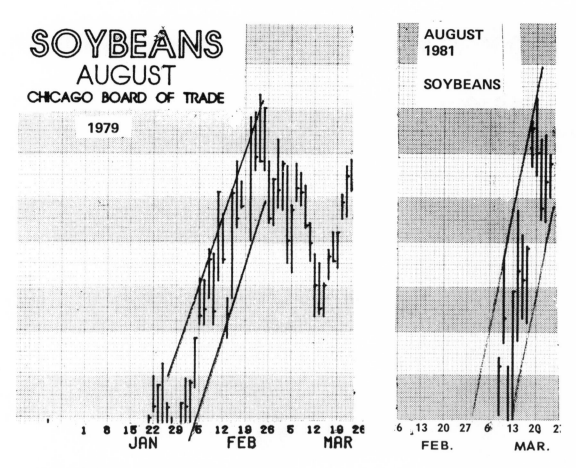

Chart furnished courtesy Commodity Perspective

FIGURE 61
CORN REPEATING CHANNELS

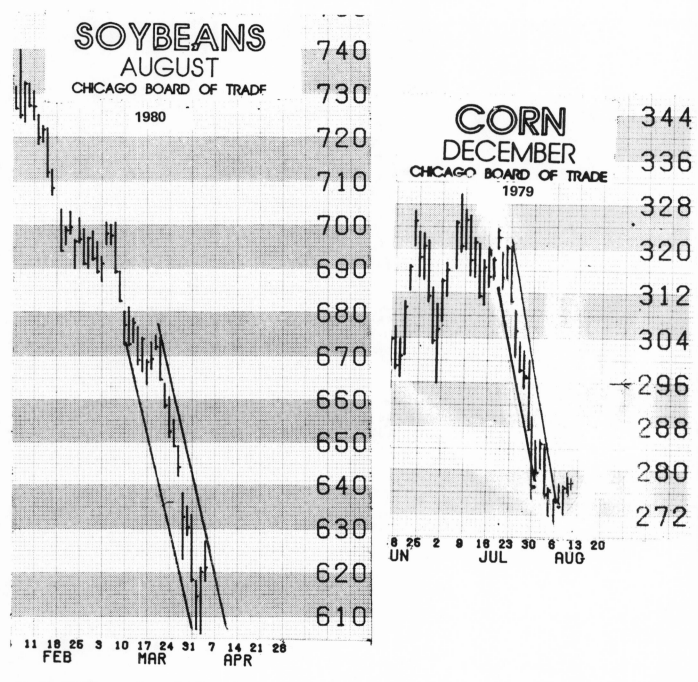

Chart furnished courtesy Commodity Perspective

162

FIGURE 62
CATTLE REPEATING CHANNELS

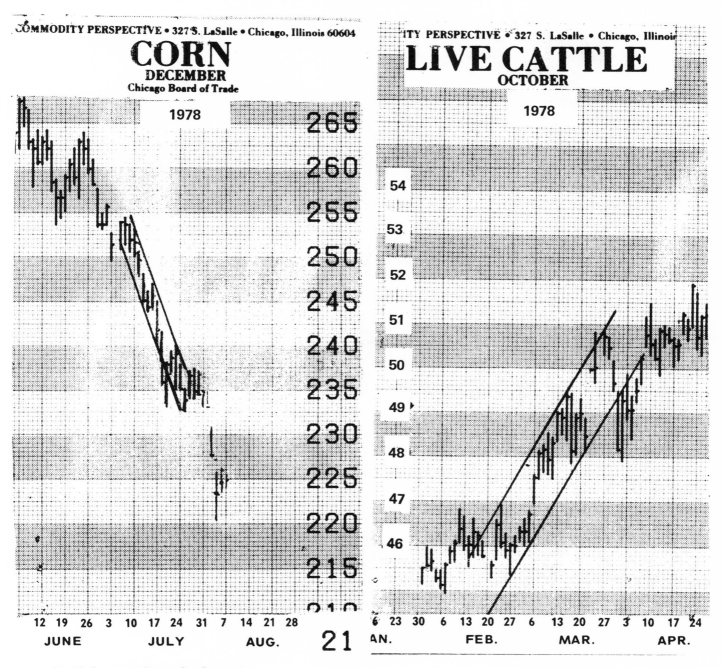

Chart furnished courtesy Commodity Perspective

163

FIGURE 63

CATTLE REPEATING CHANNELS

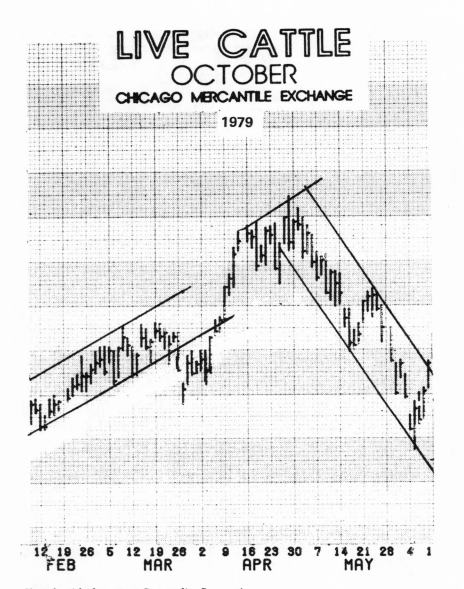

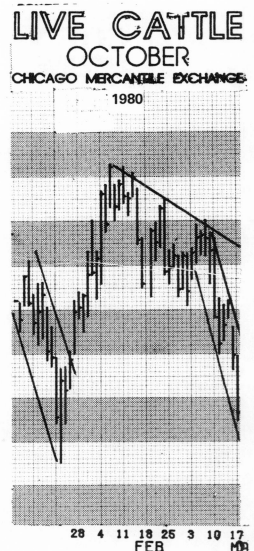

Chart furnished courtesy Commodity Perspective

on Figure 58. The marks at the bottom are the short cycle time periods. Note how swing B3 had a congestion at the cycle time. The swing size and angle within the cycle time period help the short term trader.

2. It is important to know at what slope the commodity is traveling. This can be found fast and easy, without cluttering the chart, by using a widget with the degree angles off a base line. The angles to be used are: 1) 22 degrees; 2) 33 degrees; 3) 45 degrees; 4) 62 degrees; 5) 72 degrees. This gives the boundaries within which the price may stay before being considered a change (see Figure 64). Use these categories in making comparisons. This way short numbers may be used for reference. For example, M3 may be logged as the main angle in the forty-five degree category. M3-C4 can mean that the main angle is in three while the cycle angle is in four. It is important to be able to have standard abbreviations to help speed up your analysis. The rate of change can be shown by putting the previous price category in brackets. For example, M4-(M5)-C4 can mean that the angle has changed recently from seventy degrees to the sixty-two degree category within the short cycle time span. When desiring to estimate the size of the down angle, further help may be recorded quickly by having this information coded in the formula such as M4-(M5)-C4/C4 + 10, which indicates that the angle, when the market reverses, should be ten degrees more than the C4 angle when it turns.

The widget made of transparent material should have the base line even with the perpendicular time lines of the chart and the "zero" point at the turn. See below for illustrations:

(NOT TO SCALE)

WIDGET

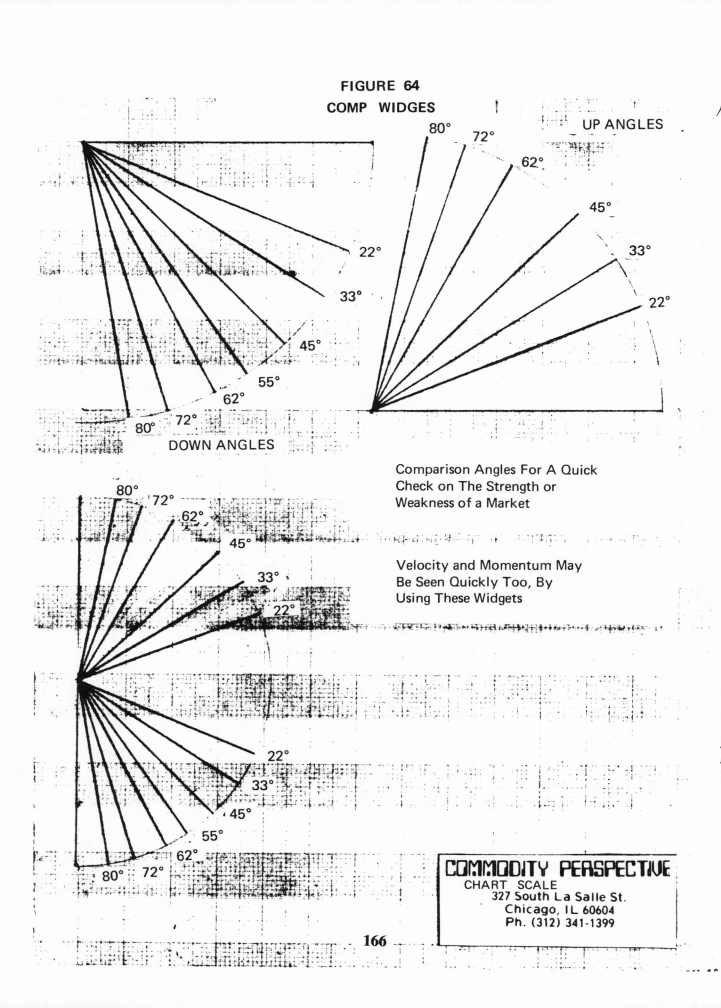

FIGURE 64
COMP WIDGES

UP ANGLES

80° 72° 62° 45° 33° 22°

22° 33° 45° 55° 62° 72° 80°

DOWN ANGLES

Comparison Angles For A Quick
Check on The Strength or
Weakness of a Market

Velocity and Momentum May
Be Seen Quickly Too, By
Using These Widgets

80° 72° 62° 45° 33° 22°

22° 33° 45° 55° 62° 72° 80°

COMMODITY PERSPECTIVE
CHART SCALE
327 South La Salle St.
Chicago, IL 60604
Ph. (312) 341-1399

166

3. Special note should be made as to whether or not the line of travel is above or below the middle lines. In an up market, the forty-five degree or middle is considered normal, the twenty-two degree weak, and the sixty degree strong. In a down market everything is about ten degrees more, so that seventy degrees instead of sixty is considered strong; the fifty-five normal; and the thirty or less considered weak. An extra widget can be made for down markets. The level and stage of the market makes a difference. Divergence from the normal is the important thing to find.

4. When making comparisons over several years, the level and stage of each market must be compared. No one should expect the same angles on a low priced bottoming market as on a high priced topping market.

5. Expect the rule of alternates to work. If there has been a zig-zag pattern, a flat or irregular may be coming up next. Use Elliott wave pattern recognition techniques

HOW TO TELL A STRONG MOVE

1. The angle is sharper.
2. The angle is above the average angle line.
3. Time price ratios are on schedule (or ahead).
4. The reactions are only two days or less; and the first congestion area is small.

FINDING THE WEAK MOVE

1. The angle of travel is below the middle line or forty-five degrees.
2. There are occasional collapses to the twenty-two degree or less range, or perhaps back to base-line support.
3. Time is in balance with price. This is working from a previous longer term move.
4. Price just hangs in a zone, with time running out.

FINDING AVERAGE ANGLES

The price level makes a difference in the average angle. Near historical lows the angles are usually flatter and at old highs, the angles are usually sharper. Each commodity has its own characteristics. They each must be studied individually and understood in comparison with the factors affecting them.

Ordinarily, the angle going down is sharper than that going up, but with some commodities this is not true. For example, pork bellies will usually go up and down on about the same angle. Wheat will usually go down slower than it goes up, if you consider the short thrusts characterized by wheat. Angles are not considered in congestion areas, although these short swings are often the same here too; but our research skipped them for the most part.

When angles change they often do so on the same increments for a market. For example, it may start up on a thirty degree angle when down at historical lows, then change to a sixty as it goes out of the bottoming patterns. The velocity is shown by the degree of the angle. High velocity at low levels is suspect and should be considered accumulation indications. Low velocity at high levels indicates that the bulls are leery and the bears are not ready to make their move.

We have been using Commodity Perspective charts and have tried to adjust for the changes in scale found in these charts. Each person should do his own work to see for himself how this works. If he can get charts all on the same scale with an .001 precision, he will do better. Velocity is only good when compared with what previous speed has been. With some practice the speed comparisons can be made very rapidly, especially if transparent overlays are made. Look for deviations from the normal. When things do not do what they normally would do, this is important. Below are close approximations of average angles under various circumstances. Sometimes the average angle will change to another and then come back to the first average angle. Some commodities are more erratic than others. The information following should help, but do not exclusively use this information. Do your own work! The latest average angle takes precedence over the past.

AVERAGE ANGLES

		(degrees) UP	(degrees) DOWN
1)	Soy Beans		
	May	75	80
	1978		
	Nov.	65	65
	May	75	85
	1979		
	Nov.	75	85
	May	80	77
	1980		
	Nov.	70 (85)	70 (80)

(Beans are noted for three day thrusts, or four with overlapping days.)

2)	Pork Bellies		
	Feb.	80	80
	1978		
	Aug.	82	82
	Feb.	92	75
	1979		
	Aug.	85	85
	Feb.	70 (80)	70 (80)
	1980		
	Aug.	75	75

3)	Corn		
	July	67	80
	1978		
	Dec.	65 (82)	65 (82)
	July	70	60
	1979		
	Dec.	70	60
	July	80	85
	1980		
	Dec.	80	85

4)	Cattle		
	April	45	75
	1978		
	Dec	45	75

(There were some sharp up thrusts but they came sharply back.)

	April	75	45 (75)
	1979		
	Dec.	50	77

(1979 cattle was rather irregular.)

	April	85 (80)	80
	1980		
	Dec.	75 (85)	80 (85)

Numbers in brackets ( ) means this is for short thrusts

AVERAGE ANGLES (continued)

		(degrees) UP	(degrees) DOWN
5)	Hogs		
	June	70	80
	1978		
	Dec.	80	80
	June	70	80
	1979		
	Dec.	80	80
	June	79 (80)	75 (85)
	1980		
	Dec.	70 (80)	75 (85)

(When hogs are down around 40 cents, angles are much flatter.)

6)	D-Mark			
	1978	June	80	80
	1979	June	60 (80)	60 (75)

(Not too consistent this year)

7)	T-Bills		
	June	75	85
	1978		
	Dec.	75	85
	June	85	75
	1979		
	Dec.	80	70
	June	60 (77)	75 (80)
	1980		
	Dec.	80	80 (70)

8)	Lumber			
	1978	Sept.	80	82
	1979	Sept.	80	80
		May	55 (77)	75
	1980			
		Nov.	80	70

(Lumber is not very regular. Angles change more often.)

9)	Wheat			
	July		82	82
	1978			
	Dec.		85	80
	May		(85)	(84) (short thrusts)

(This was flat until April.)

1979			
Dec.	80	75	
July	85 (85)	75 (82)	
1980			
Dec.	60 (85)	55 (80)	

The velocity is found by the changes of angles. If there is a thirty percent change of angle, there is a thirty percent change in velocity.

Long term angles will be different in many cases. For example, 1980 December Wheat went up long term on close to a 40 degree angle.

REPEATING SWINGS

1. Introduction

In most commodities several swing sizes repeat four or five times in a short period and even as many as eight or ten times on occasion. Knowing these repetitious swings gives a trader the advantage. The swing, or leg, is measured from its bottom tip to the top tip of a turning point in market action. Angle size may be sharp or flat, but the measurement is from bottom of pivot to top point where it turns down.

2. Boundaries and Measuring Conditions

Where changes are most apt to occur may not be at the beginning or end of a contract. The time of year does not have too much significance, although some seasonal factors may occur. These swings may keep reoccurring, then something may happen to cause a burst of energy in the market and bring on a lot more activity. With the increased volatility, there usually develops a new set of repeating swings. With some commodities, the repeating swings may go for several years, alternating for only short periods.

There is usually a short swing, followed by another about twice this size, but the swings may increase about one-half more than either of these. The same length change in a swing often occurs. For example, the swing may be one-half inch in the beginning, go to one and a half inches, then two and one-half inches, with an inch increase each time.

Runaway markets skip the small swings, making larger ones about like the middle size ones found in a slower market with less volatility. Some commodities are more erratic than others. Thin markets have less reliability.

We used Commodity Perspective charts to do our measuring. They change their scaling occasionally, but we adjusted our measurements accordingly. More accurate averages may be obtained with charts that keep consistent scaling.

171

Angle Average Trading

We think these are close enough to help a trader, in spite of the chart scale changes and the problems this causes. Traders should do their own work on this, however, to get a feel of the market and to learn the characteristics of each commodity they expect to trade.

3. Possible Cause for Differences and Changes in Repeating Swing Sizes
    a. Level of price or top and bottom price level characteristics.
    b. Trade participation or amount of open interest.
    c. Accumulation or distribution activity.
    d. Newsy markets.
        1) Rumors and speculation on market changing events.
        2) Weather conditions.
        3) Strikes or political turmoil.

REPEATER SWING SIZES

			Small	Next	Next	Next
1)	Beans					
		Nov.	1"	1¼"	2"	
	1978					
		May	1"	1"	2½"	
		Nov.	13/16"	1 9/16"	none found	
	1979					
		May	1"	1½"	3 1/8"	
		Nov.	1"	1¾"	3 1/8"	
	1980					
		May	¾"	1¾"	3"	
2)	Bellies					
		Aug.	1"	2"	4"	
	1978	Feb				
		Feb.	¾"	1 5/8"	3½"	
		Aug.	2"	none found	4"	
	1979					
		Feb.	1"	2½"	3½"	
		Aug.	1"	1¾"	3 5/8"	
	1980					
		Feb.	1"	1 5/9"	3 5/8"	

172

			Small	Next	Next	Next
3)	Cattle					
	1978	Dec.	¾"	1¼"	2¼"	
		June	¾"	1 1/8"	3"	
	1979	Dec.	¾"	1½"	2¼"	
		June	13/16"	1 5/8"	4"	
	1980	Dec.	1¼"	2¼"	none found	
		June	5/8"	1½"	3¾"	
4)	Corn					
	1978	July	¾"	1¾"	3½"	
		Dec.	½"	1"	1¾"	
	1979	July	1"	2"	3"	
		Dec.	½"	1"	1¾"	
	1980	July	1¼"	1¾"	3½"	
		Dec.	½"	1¼"	1¾"	
5)	Hogs					
	1978	July	1"	1 3/8"	3 3/8	
		Dec.	1 5/16"	2 1/8"	none found	
	1979	July	¾"	1 15/16"	3¼"	
		Dec.	1"	1½"	none found	
	1980	July	½"	1,"	1 13/16"	2 1/16"
		Dec.	1"	1½"	none found	
6)	Lumber					
	1978	Mar.	13/16"	1½"	2 15/16"	
		Sept.	½";;	13/16"	1½"	
	1979	Mar.	3/4"	1½"	none found	
	1980	Sept.	1¼"	1½"	2"	2 3/8"

Lumber is not consistent with its repeaters. They do not continue as long as others, and sizes may vary more often. Contract months did not change this pattern, but there is enough repetition to help those who need to trade this market.

173

		Small	Next	Next	Next
7) T-Bills					
	June	1 5/16''	1 11/16''	2½''	
1978					
	Dec.	½'' & ¾''	1¼''	2 3/8''	3¼''
	June	11/16''	2''	2 5/16''	
1979					
	Dec.	½'' & ¾''	1''	2''	4''
	June	5/8''&1''	1¼''	2''	2 5/16''
1980					
	Dec.	½'' & ¾''	1¾''	2¾''	3¾''
8) Wheat					
	July	7/8''	1 5/8''	3''	4 1/8''
1978					
	Dec.	1''	1¾''	2 3/16''	
	July	1¼''	2½''	4½''	
1979					
	Dec.	1''	1½''	2½;;	
	July	7/8''	1½''	3½''	
1980					
	Dec.	1''	1¾''	2 3/16''	

(December averages out at one, one and three-quarters, and two inches.)

174

FIGURE 65
HAP TIME AND PRICE WIDGET

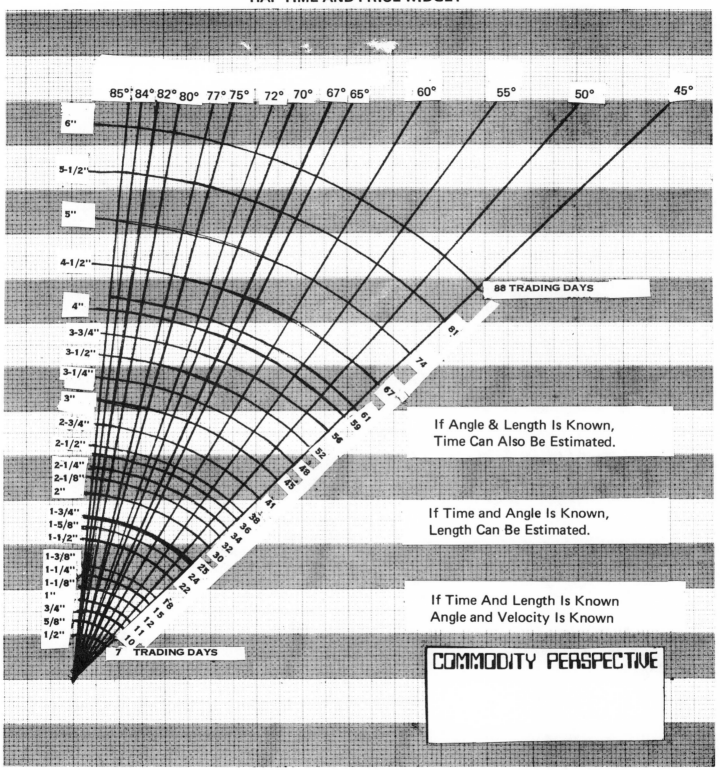

If Angle & Length Is Known,
Time Can Also Be Estimated.

If Time and Angle Is Known,
Length Can Be Estimated.

If Time And Length Is Known
Angle and Velocity Is Known

COMMODITY PERSPECTIVE

FIGURE 66
HAP T & P UP ANGLE WIDGET

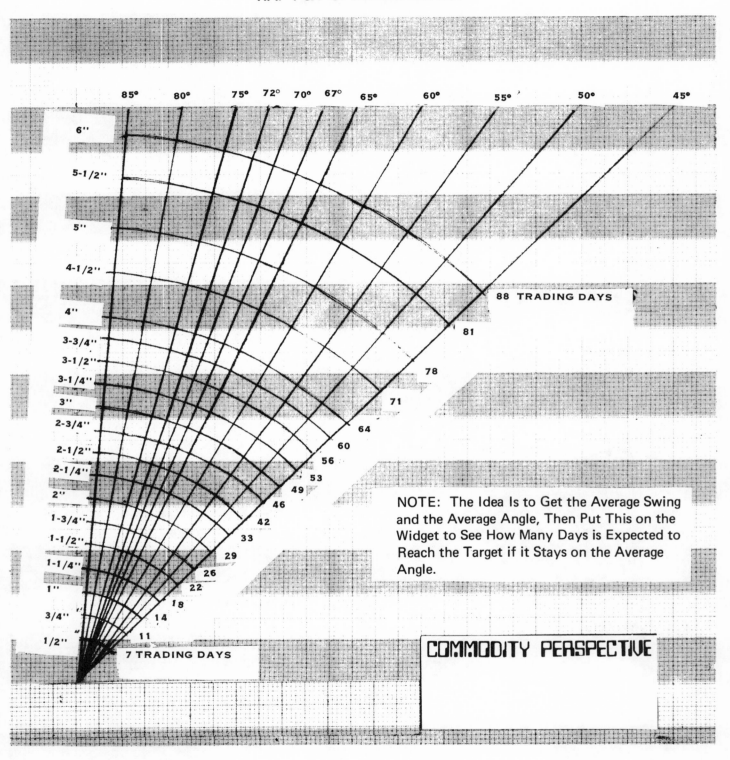

NOTE: The Idea Is to Get the Average Swing and the Average Angle, Then Put This on the Widget to See How Many Days is Expected to Reach the Target if it Stays on the Average Angle.

COMMODITY PERSPECTIVE

176

FIGURE 67

HAP T & P DOWN ANGLE WIDGET

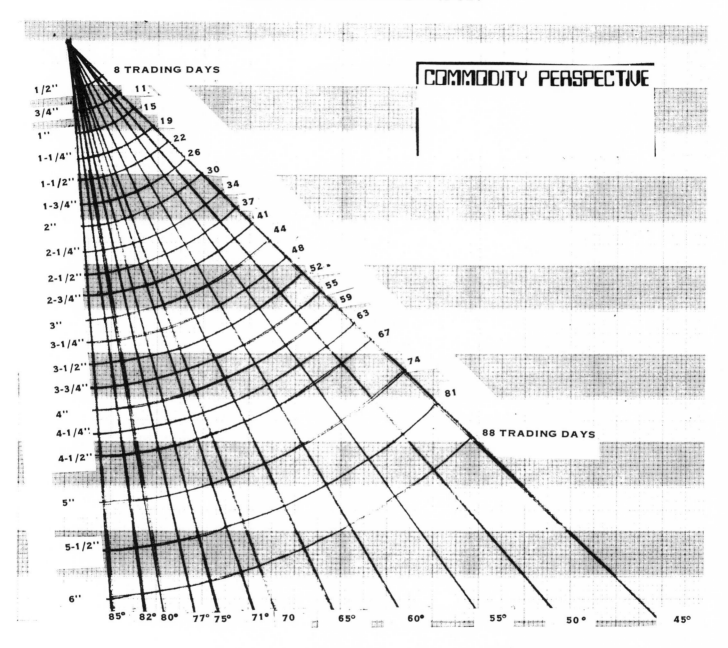

NOTE: These must be remade by each trader to understand their real significance. The left column are the average swing lengths taken from our work labeled "repeater size swings" starting on Page 172. The count of the days begins from the point at the top. There are five days in each main division. Count over horizontally then come down vertically until you reach the point of swing size and angle amount.

WAYS TO USE THE AVERAGE ANGLES

1. A Momentum Indicator
The degree of travel tells how fast or slow the market is moving and how long it will take to reach a target. Flatter angles will get to a destination slower, or perhaps not at all if time limitations are involved. Comparisons with the middle line and previous average angles will tell the speed of the present move.

Note how the congestion at "w" on the chart of Live Cattle (Figure 58) pulled the angle over. Lines from "w" to 4, "x" to 5, and "y" to 6 would be the average short term cycle size up angle. The lines from B to 4, C to 5, D to 6 take in three of the short term cycles and give another comparison. When price was coming down, the 4D line stopped at Y, but was expected to go to 5. When it went up on a sharper than normal angle from X, it was expected to pull back or go sideways until averaging out.

2. Price Projection
Average angle methods help in finding the target. See how this is used in the chaper called, "Hit the Target."

3. Use in Trading
a. Draw a parallel of the average angle out from the last pivot either up or down, according to the trend of the market. Stay in the market as long as price is even or above this line on a bull move or below this line on a bear move. Either way price should be to the left of the line. Go off each pivot with the commodity's average angle.

b. Make lines up (or down) from congestions after a breakout for use in judging the strength of the market.

c. If taken out prematurely, reenter by these methods:

1) In a zig-zag price pattern when the previous day's low is passed in a down market, or the previous high in an up market.

2) For flat and irregular price patterns, wait for the second previous day's highs or lows before reentering.

d. Stay in until price comes back through the average angle line.

WHY THIS IS IMPORTANT

1. Recognize momentum easier.
2. Avoid false reversals more often.
3. Obtain price targets to help in money control.

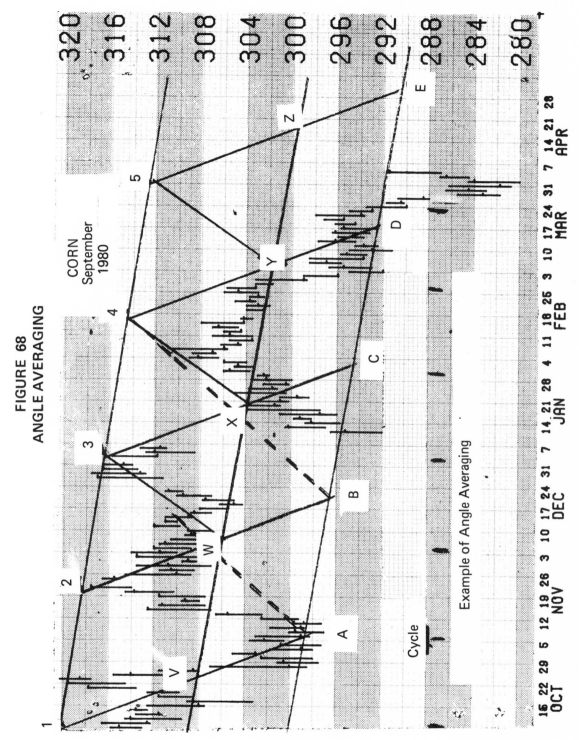

FIGURE 68
ANGLE AVERAGING

CORN
September
1980

Example of Angle Averaging

Chart furnished courtesy Commodity Perspective

179

HOW TO USE THIS INFORMATION

1. The amount an angle travels above or below normal, going up, will often tell what to expect going down.

2. A long sharp angle will usually produce a sharp reversal, or a flat short angle will produce a broader reversal.

3. The latest average angles are the most important for trading.

4. Use older averages for momentum comparisons.

5. Have each commodity's record and characteristics well known.

6. Put the angle on the last pivot and stay in until the line has been crossed.

PREDICTING REVERSALS

1. When a larget area is hit, stops should be brought up close because a reversal is expected.

2. When time and price balance, a reversal is expected (see Figure 69).

3. When corrections are larger than normal, suspect a change of trend.

4. When Pivot Finder lines are hit, a change should come.

5. When old highs or lows are reached watch for a pivot.

6. When there is the third change of an angle of travel of a move, expect a reversal.

7. When the momentum of a reversal is greater than the previous, or if there is an angle of reversal much sharper than was expected, expect a change.

8. Use Elliott count to help with price patterns. Know when the move started and how it has progressed; and most important, what stage is presently positioned.

THEORY THAT LOOKS GOOD

Checking back over a lot of charts, and adding up the amount of angle degrees in each move, gives evidence that there is an average number of degrees in a movement of the market. Further work is being done to verify this theory, but so far the results have been favorable. This gives the ability to know the approximate number of turns expected for a move to reach the average number of degrees simply by adding angles in previous turns. Problems arise in deciding where to start adding the degrees and size of a move to use in adding the degree amounts. So far there is evidence that when the main trend makes a correction then resumes on a different angle, the new angle is expected to be sharper with price moving up faster (see Figure 70).

PROBLEMS INVOLVED WITH
THE ANGLE AVERAGING METHOD

1. Find the congestion areas. There can be some loss of earnings if a congestion area turns up where it is not expected. Use the congestion-area finding techniques of HAP to help here. The worst that should happen is to lose some profits in a move, since there should not be any positioning at this late date.

2. There are times when the angle lines slide over to a lower level or creep up to a higher level. This may be a problem. These should be watched to see if they stay on the same angle trend line. Going up will not hurt when below the angle line will probably result in a correction or congestion area (See Figure 71 for an illustration).

USING MOVING AVERAGES TO TRADE
THE ANGLE COMPARISONS

1. First make a moving average about the same size as the number of days in an average swing. Second, take one-half the number of days in the average leg found (with the averaging of back prices) and make a moving average of the closing prices; third, take one quarter the number of days and make a moving average. You will end up with three moving averages. For example, if the average number of days in a move for the commodity is. twelve days, there would be a twelve, six, and three-day moving average. On the three-day, or shortest term moving average, leave an "x" at each new entry to see distances apart and judge momentum.

181

FIGURE 69

BALANCING TIME AND PRICE WITH FIBONACCI NUMBERS

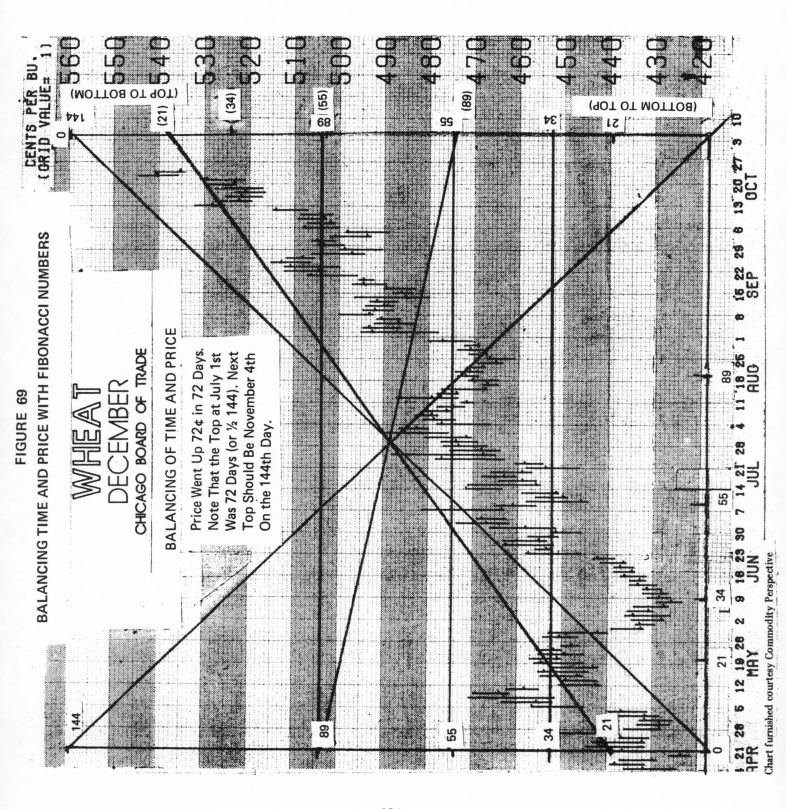

WHEAT
DECEMBER
CHICAGO BOARD OF TRADE

BALANCING OF TIME AND PRICE

Price Went Up 72¢ in 72 Days.
Note That the Top at July 1st
Was 72 Days (or ½ 144). Next
Top Should Be November 4th
On the 144th Day.

CENTS PER BU.
(GRID VALUE = 1)

(TOP TO BOTTOM)

(BOTTOM TO TOP)

Chart furnished courtesy Commodity Perspective

FIGURE 70
CHANGE OF ANGLE

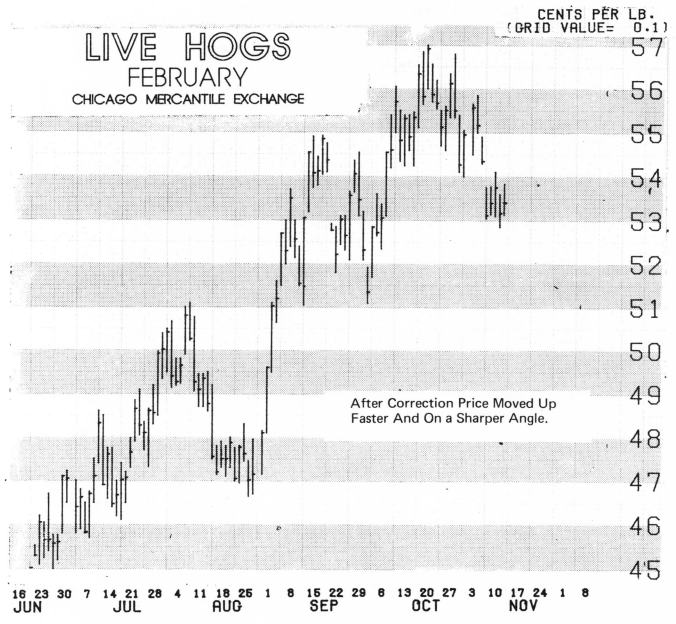

CENTS PER LB.
(GRID VALUE= 0.1)

LIVE HOGS
FEBRUARY
CHICAGO MERCANTILE EXCHANGE

After Correction Price Moved Up
Faster And On a Sharper Angle.

57
56
55
54
53
52
51
50
49
48
47
46
45

16 23 30 7 14 21 28 4 11 18 25 1 8 15 22 29 6 13 20 27 3 10 17 24 1 8
JUN   JUL   AUG   SEP   OCT   NOV

Chart furnished courtesy Commodity Perspective

183

2. Draw trend lines along the "x's" of the three-day moving average to conform with the channel lines of the move, hitting as many of the "x's" as possible.

3. Contraction (when the middle and three-day moving average begin to get closer together) reveals price is losing momentum; when the lines spread apart, this indicates that momentum is speeding up.

4. When price is above the channel "x" line, this indicates that it is proceeding properly; when price closes on the other side of the channel "x" line, this means that it is losing momentum and will soon stall out. Order and rhythm should be seen in the contractions and expansions of the moving average (see Figure 72).

5. Put the average angle line on the main turning points of the middle MA line (using the averaged leg amount). When price comes to this averaged angle line, it should hold. If it does not, suspect a reversal (see Figure 71).

6. The way the "x" trend line is skewed in a relationship with the averaged angle line keeps one posted on the way the market is gaining or losing strength.

7. If price penetrates the small moving average line and closes here, it is expected to go on to the next moving average line. If it does not, this is a failure and shows renewed strength.

HOW TO USE ANGLE AVERAGES

The theory behind this is that most people are usually wrong. Most people cannot accurately judge fundamental or technical aspects of the market. Finding the average line of travel, the average speed of travel and the average length of travel reveals the normal thinking about a commodity. Above this normal or below this normal is overdoing or underdoing it. But should the market get to the estimated target twice as fast, it is apt to pull back sooner than expected. If it is fifty percent below normal in speed, it will take twice as long to get to target. Look for a market that stays on a normal run or slightly above it. If it is too far above, it probably will pull back quicker. Knowing the rate of speed and the expected time or target area should help make profits.

FIGURE 71

SLIDING TO LOWER AVERAGE ANGLE

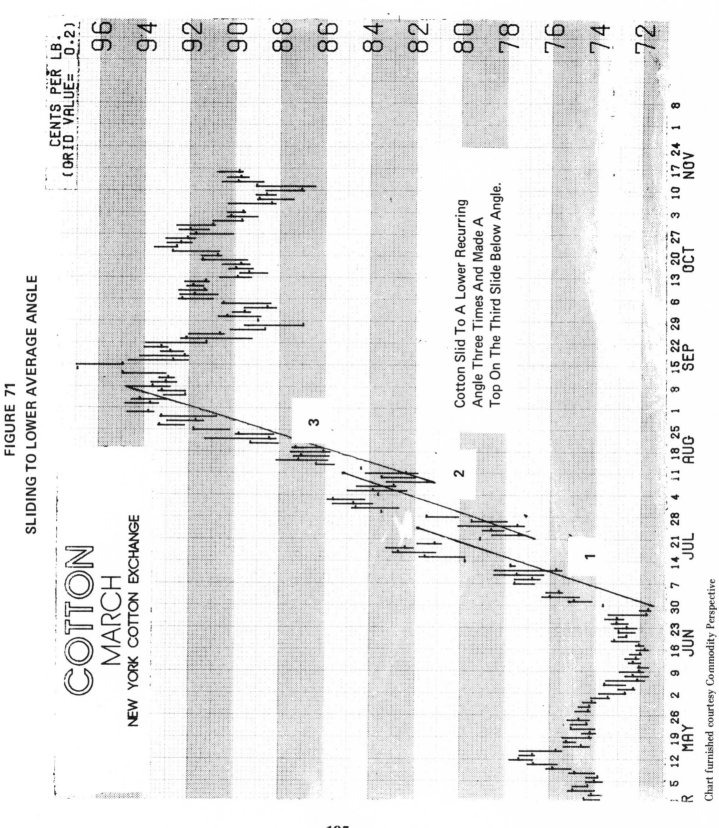

COTTON
MARCH
NEW YORK COTTON EXCHANGE

CENTS PER LB.
(GRID VALUE= 0.2)

Cotton Slid To A Lower Recurring
Angle Three Times And Made A
Top On The Third Slide Below Angle.

Chart furnished courtesy Commodity Perspective

185

FIGURE 72

THREE MOVING AVERAGES WITH AVERAGE ANGLE CHANNELS

**THREE MOVING AVERAGES
USED WITH AVERAGE ANGLES.
(SHOWN HERE)**

The three, six, and twelve day moving averages were used because they were the average number of days in swings, or average swing lengths. Note the expansions and contractions denoting strength or weakness.

Pay particular attention to the "X" line and the distances apart. Unusually close or far apart denotes momentum changes. Clusters or sideways action on these "X" lines shows congestion.

The Average angles coming off of turning points were almost on the middle moving average much of the time.

The Angle averages were found by going to the charts of our research found above.

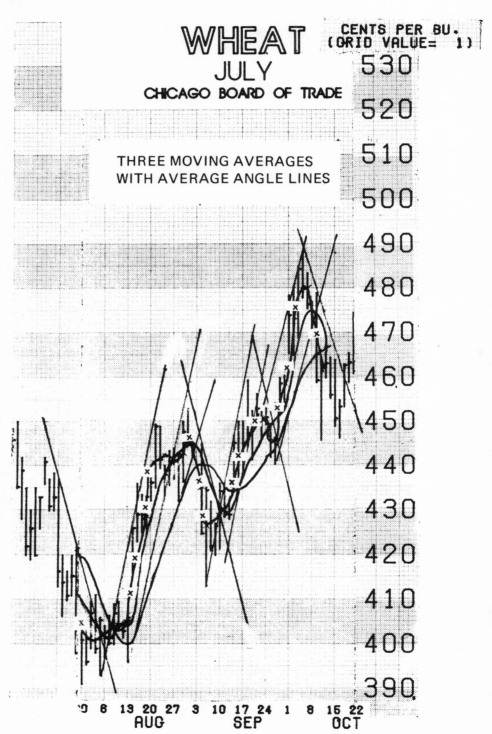

FINDING THE TARGET

Know the average swing length by estimation of previous similar markets. Use channels, cycles, rhythm, and time-price balancing.

FIND VOLATILITY

Know the average angle of travel, the average amplitude, and the amplitude of previous similar markets to see if the present price is above or below the average.

USING THIS INFORMATION

Make a set of scaled transparent overlays showing various lengths of a move at various speeds. Have these in increments the same as the movement of the market involved. Keep these handy to know when a market is ready to give some profits.

WHY THIS WILL WORK

This puts the odds in the favor of the user. Even if the movements of the market should be random; when runs go above the average in one direction or the other, this reveals which way to trade with the majority on your side.

Data Used For Moving Averages Shown On July Wheat Chart Along With Average Angles

DATE	OPEN	HIGH	LOW	CLOSE	3 DAY	6 DAY	12 DAY
730	393.00	402.50	391.00	401.00	407.17	410.50	420.58
731	403.00	403.00	395.50	396.00	400.67	407.08	418.08
801	403.00	409.50	399.00	407.00	401.33	405.92	417.00
802	411.00	411.00	398.00	399.00	400.67	403.92	41417
803	398.00	406.00	393.00	405.50	403.83	402.25	411.21
806	400.00	404.00	397.00	401.50	402.00	401.67	408.75
807	401.00	406.50	400.00	400.25	402.42	401.54	406.02
808	401.25	409.00	400.00	407.00	402.92	403.38	405.23
809	409.50	409.50	403.00	404.00	403.75	402.88	404.40
810	405.00	405.00	401.50	403.00	404.67	403.54	403.73
813	396.50	406.00	396.00	406.00	404.33	403.63	402.94
814	425.00	426.00	416.00	426.00	411.67	407.71	404.69
815	424.00	436.00	423.00	429.00	420.33	412.50	407.02
816	427.50	433.50	425.00	429.00	428.00	416.17	409.77
817	430.50	433.00	426.00	433.00	430.33	421.00	411.94
820	433.50	437.50	430.00	436.25	432.75	426.54	415.04
821	436.00	449.50	435.00	449.00	439.42	433.71	418.67
822	449.00	449.00	439.50	441.50	442.25	436.29	422.00
823	437.00	440.00	433.50	438.00	442.83	437.79	425.15
824	437.50	443.50	435.50	441.00	440.17	439.79	427.98
827	440.00	444.00	437.50	441.00	440.00	441.13	431.06
828	439.00	443.00	432.00	442.75	441.58	442.21	434.38
829	440.00	450.00	436.50	447.75	443.83	442.00	437.85
830	452.00	453.00	447.00	449.50	446.67	443.33	439.81
831	445.50	447.00	442.50	444.75	447.33	444.46	441.13
904	445.00	445.00	424.75	424.75	439.67	441.75	440.77
905	421.50	435.00	413.00	434.50	434.67	440.67	440.90
906	429.00	432.00	421.00	422.00	427.08	437.21	429.71
907	420.50	427.00	420.00	426.50	427.67	433.67	437.83
910	425.00	436.00	421.50	434.25	427.58	431.13	437.23
911	433.00	436.00	428.50	429.00	429.92	428.50	436.48
912	428.00	433.00	428.00	429.00	430.75	429.21	435.48
913	434.50	447.00	434.00	445.25	434.42	431.00	435.83
914	440.00	450.00	437.50	441.50	438.58	434.25	435.73
917	439.00	450.00	439.00	445.25	444.00	437.38	435.52
918	449.50	459.50	444.50	447.50	444.75	439.58	435.35
919	445.00	452.50	441.50	450.00	447.58	443.08	435.79
920	452.00	456.50	450.00	453.00	450.17	447.08	438.15
921	449.00	452.25	446.50	450.75	451.25	448.00	439.50
924	452.00	453.00	449.50	451.00	451.58	449.58	441.92
925	448.50	449.50	442.00	445.50	449.08	449.63	443.50
926	443.50	446.50	440.50	446.25	447.58	449.42	444.50
927	454.50	460.00	451.50	458.75	450.17	450.88	446.98
928	460.00	460.50	454.50	458.50	454.50	451.79	449.44
1001	470.00	478.50	465.50	474.00	463.75	455.67	451.83
1002	475.00	480.50	465.00	473.25	468.58	459.38	454.48
1003	470.50	485.00	469.00	484.50	477.25	465.88	457.75
1004	479.00	488.50	478.00	480.50	479.42	471.58	460.50
1005	481.00	483.50	475.50	476.50	480.50	474.54	462.71
1008	472.50	477.00	471.00	474.75	427.25	477.25	464.52
1009	477.50	479.00	459.00	459.50	470.25	474.83	465.25
1010	460.50	464.50	446.00	461.50	465.25	472.88	466.13
1011	461.00	465.50	461.00	463.25	461.42	469.33	467.60
1012	462.00	464.50	456.25	456.25	460.33	465.29	468.44

References

Action-Reaction — F.F.E.S., Dr. A.H. Andrews Sr., 538 S.W. 53 Terrace, S. Miami, Florida 33155

Commodity Trading Systems and Methods, R.J. Kaufman, John Wiley & Sons, 605 Third Ave., New York, N.Y. 10158

Complete Writings of R.N. Elliott, Commodity Research Institute, Box 1866, Hendersonville, North Carolina 28739

Commodity Yearbook, 1980, Commodity Research Bureau, Inc., One Liberty Plaza, New York, N.Y. 10006

Six Self-Made Millionaires, Commodition Associates, Box 876, Phoenix, Arizona 85001

Congestion Phase System, Eugene Nofri, Box 1995, Santa Monica, California 90406

How I Made $1,000,000 Trading Commodities Last Year, by Larry Williams, Windsor Books, Box 280, Brightwaters, New York 11718

How To Make Money in the Futures Market, Charles Drummond, Box 958 Station Q, Toronto, Ontario, Canada M4T 2P1

How To Make Profits Trading in Commodities, W.D. Gann, 1942, Lambert-Gann Publishing Co., Inc., Box O, Pomeroy, Washington 99347

Making It in the Market, Richard Ney, 1975, McGraw-Hill Books, 1221 Ave. of Americas, New York, N.Y. 10020

Making Money in Cotton, Burton Pugh, Lambert-Gann Publishing Co., Inc., Box O, Pomeroy, Washington 99347

Ohama's 3-D Concept, 166 North Canon Dr., Beverly Hills, California 90210

Reminiscences of a Stock Operator, Edwin LeFevre, 1923, Doubleday & Co., Inc., Garden City, N.Y. 11530

Scientific Interpretation of Bar Charts, John R. Hill, Box 1866, Hendersonville, North Carolina 28739

Textbook on the Wave Principle, Investment Educators, 1426 West Cullon, Chicago, Illinois 60613